# ADVICE TO
# CLEVER CHILDREN

This book is published by Oxford Forum, based in Cuddesdon near Oxford. We are a group of dissident academics, aiming to set up an independent university supported by business enterprises.

Information about us can be found on our website: **www.celiagreen.com**

We welcome temporary workers, whether or not interested in the possibility of a career with us. School-leavers and those in higher education could come for holiday jobs or something more long-term. We are also interested in forming associations with those in or approaching retirement.

People in the modern world are encouraged to seek feedback from doing something 'creative', and from the social status and power over other people which a job may provide. On such terms we cannot hope to compete. Nevertheless, we are perhaps the only organisation still promoting standards and values being eliminated by the reductionist worldview that is now dominant.

Anyone who came to work with us would very likely be able to accelerate our progress considerably.

Dr Celia Green
Director
Oxford Forum

# ADVICE TO
# CLEVER CHILDREN

CELIA GREEN

*First published in Great Britain, 1981*
*by Institute of Psychophysical Research, Oxford*
*Phototypeset in V.I.P. Garamond by*
*Western Printing Services Ltd, Bristol*
*and printed in Great Britain at*
*The Pitman Press, Bath*
*ISBN 0 900076 07 0*

# Contents

# Acknowledgements

Acknowledgements are due to the following for permission to quote from copyright material in the books indicated: Allen & Unwin Ltd. – J. R. R. Tolkien, *The Lord of the Rings*; Benn Bros. Ltd. – H. G. Wells, *The Apple* in *Complete Short Stories*; Collins Sons & Co. Ltd. – C. S. Lewis, *The Pilgrim's Regress*; Doubleday & Co. Inc. – R. M. Grant and D. N. Freedman, *The Secret Sayings of Jesus*; Darton, Longman & Todd Ltd. – William Hamilton, *The New Essence of Christianity*; Macmillan & Co. Ltd. – Charles Morgan, *Sparkenbroke*, Sir James Frazer, *The Golden Bough*; Penguin Books Ltd. – John Allegro, *The Dead Sea Scrolls*; The Philadelphia Bulletin – Charlton Ogburn, 'Torture par Correspondance'; S.C.M. Press Ltd. – Paul Tillich, *The Shaking of the Foundations*; Routledge & Kegan Paul Ltd. – C. S. Nott, *Teachings of Gurdjieff*. Detailed references will be found with each quotation.

# Introduction

Dearly beloved children, in this world they will tell you all sorts of things. And what is indeed more to the point, they will imply even more things than they say. This world is filled with pitfalls for the unwary.

This book is a small guide to pitfalls. I am uniquely qualified to write it, because once I was a clever child myself. This world is enriched with a particularly plenteous supply of pitfalls for clever children (whom it hates, unless they take care to become stupid) so I have become an expert on pitfalls. Perhaps I am the only expert. Everyone else has fallen in.

*

I taught myself to read when I was eighteen months old, although my parents did not find out until just after my second birthday. I was, of course, in all respects very precocious.

It appears that my parents managed to avoid noticing that I could read until after my second birthday; I suppose it is more respectable to discover such a thing when your child is two rather than before it is. So they ascribed my interest in books and comics only to the pictures. But in fact it seems that I paid great attention to the written word from my first birthday onwards, and my own first memory of reading seems to require to be dated before I was twenty months old. Even if this memory is discounted, when I was eventually found to be able to read, I was fluent and proficient, so it is scarcely plausible that I was a beginner.

It is, these days, not fashionable to want your child to be a prodigy. It is supposed to be the case that there is some great danger in 'pushing' a child, and none whatever in holding it back. So my parents, thoroughly imbued with these notions, considered themselves very wise in bringing me up as much as possible as if they had not noticed that I differed from the average, and brushing aside (for example) my earnest demands when I was four to learn a lot of languages.

The modern tendency to magnify and distort any appearance of disagreement between parent and child is so great that I feel some reluctance whenever I find myself mentioning that my parents' attitude to my education was, in fact, somewhat different from what I would ideally have liked. But, being realistic, it is difficult to avoid mentioning it.

However, I do not regard this as something for which they were in any way to blame. Apart from any specific pressures which were exerted on them, they had, as teachers, a keen awareness of the general climate of opinion. They knew they were likely to be accused of pushing me and concealed the age at which I learnt to read.

They were also aware of the hostility which might be aroused against me by any precocious achievement, and doubtless genuinely considered it in my best interests to try to preserve social acceptability for me by discouraging me from displaying that aggressive obsessionalism which I regarded as a natural and joyful way of living.

Even if they had wished to do the straightforward and obvious thing, and educate me in accordance with my temperament, they would no doubt have encountered bitter and headlong opposition, even sooner than they did.

In a way I think it might have been better if they had, because at least then the issues would have been in the open, although I cannot guess what the likely sequence of events would have been. But the view that human nature is so destructive that you may as well do something that provokes its open, rather than covert, hostility (supposing that something to be what you really want to do for some good reason of your own) is a highly developed cynicism of my own which I certainly do not blame my parents for not having arrived at.

There was an age limit on grammar school entrance; I suppose I would have been able to pass the grammar school scholarship when I was five, if anyone had seen fit to teach me the necessary arithmetic. As it was, I went to school dutifully from the ages of five to ten, learning next to nothing. However it fulfilled my parents' ideas of a normal childhood.

My parents apparently realised that I was finding school tedious, so they kept me away. It was a private school, so they just paid the fees, squared it with the headmistress, and I didn't go. Of course they didn't keep me away so that I could enjoy hard work and intellectual stimulus at home, I was just fairly bored at home instead of at school. But I suppose it was marginally what I would have chosen; I read the local Junior Library in a systematic way, particularly the sections labelled 'Science' and 'Adventure'. At this time, at least, this sort of hiatus did me no particular harm. I didn't have an idea of the way I wanted to be living, or of a desirable kind of intensity and progressiveness in the acquisition of knowledge, with which to compare what was actually going on. If I was bored and aimless sitting on my swing in the garden, I didn't feel guilty about it. Neither I nor anyone else was telling me that I ought to be able to make myself feel as adrenalised as if someone was teaching me advanced trigonometry for an exam in two weeks' time.

When I was ten I took the grammar school scholarship (in those days there was more flexibility in the age at which you could sit, and I took it as young as possible, qualifying by only a few weeks). I came top of the county with a hundred per cent on every paper. The next year the scholarship exam was transformed into the 11-plus. I would have had to stay in the preparatory school two years more if I had not taken it when I did, as I would not have qualified for the new age-limits until then.

When I was eleven my father got some psychologist (very experienced; his life consisted of testing school children) to do my I.Q. He said it was over 180 (but of course 180 is just the point at which it goes off the scale, and I answered everything he asked correctly). He said also that I had a phenomenal memory and added that he had never tested a child like it before, and never expected to again.

However, the same socialist government that had tightened the age-limit on the grammar school entrance had more age limits in mind, and this really ruined my academic career.

I spent the first couple of years at the grammar school learning next to nothing again, but at last (as I was continually averaging A+, which was unheard of in the history of the school) someone got the idea of pushing me up a year or so. It at once became apparent that I could mop up intellectual stuff at virtually any rate it was presented to me (when I was put up a year into a form which had done work I had not done, I immediately came top of it).

It also became apparent to me that, if I got enough intellectual input, I felt alive in a quite different sort of way, and naturally I wanted to go on having it.

Then this age limit was introduced – that you could not take School Certificate as it then was until sixteen. I was then thirteen, and in spite of having wasted the first couple of years, more or less ready to take it.

There was the most terrific dithering about whether I should take it quickly to get in before the age limit. Everyone manifested the utmost emotional disturbance at the idea of me taking it, except me, who sat working for it. I certainly wanted to take it. However, the most terrific pressure was exerted on me to get me to agree not to do so. And promises were made which certainly were not fulfilled. So I gave way, and that was the end of my compatibility with the educational system and society in general.

I may mention that by the age of thirteen my philosophical thinking was, essentially, complete. Not that it contained anything you may not find stated in one or other of the sceptical philosophers, but I thought it with a concentration and freedom from admixture which is certainly not common.

When I was twelve, the two sentences of H. G. Wells that were most sharply etched in my mind, as an expression of how I felt life should be lived, were these: 'Reality is a goddess who must be faced naked, or she ceases to bless her votaries.' 'This earth is no resting place; this earth is no playing place . . .'

And I applied these principles, relentlessly analysing any vaguely comfortable assumption that might come between the mind and the perception of the stark and enormous uncertainty in which one lived, and prepared for any effort, however strenuous, just so that it might be the most purposeful, most directly attacking thing that one could find to do.

My education was made miserable, and ultimately disastrous, by the prevailing psychological mythology. This, as one can hardly fail to be aware, includes the ideas that great harm (of an unspecified kind) can be done to children by 'pushing' them, that evil parents are sometimes ambitious for their offspring, that to achieve anything at a markedly younger age than the average is liable to set up emotional disturbances of all kinds (in the child), that nobody should be expected to work hard (particularly if they have high ability in the first place, so that the work would be likely to lead to achievement), and that there is nothing so important in life as a mysterious quality of balance, which may be roughly equated with half-heartedness.

The pantheon of myths includes no corresponding recognition that any harm can be done to anyone by holding them back, that the genuinely precocious might need to do things at a younger age than the average if their relationship to their education is not to be dislocated, that some children might be more ambitious and purposeful on their own account than their parents were for them, that some people might have an actual need to work with a certain degree of intensity in order to retain any sense of well-being, that anyone of high ability and the wrong sort of personality may expect to cause emotional disturbance in the adults around them which is liable to express itself in the most hair-raising irrationality, and that the social acceptability of putting unlimited pressure on someone to make them more 'balanced' may be offering *carte blanche* to malice and destructiveness.

The prevalence of this ideology, as expressed in the attitudes of all those around me, and in the legal structure of the educational system, was always a negative factor in my life. However, it was the legislation that made it impossible to take the School

Certificate examination before the age of sixteen that finally tilted the balance of forces definitively against me. My relationship to my education was shattered, and I was never able to restore it; although I did nothing but struggle to do so from then until the end.

When I was persuaded not to take the School Certificate that Christmas term, all the clocks of my life stopped. From then on, my education had no further significance as education, only as impossibility.

There used to be a form of execution in Africa in which a man's legs were chopped off at the knees, and he was taunted with not being able to run. I find this disgusting to think of, and I find it disgusting to think of my education in the same way.

My life, henceforward, was a nightmare. There is, as already mentioned, no prevailing wisdom to the effect that you can do anyone any harm by holding them back. I fell into the hands of socialist teachers who thought it right to exert unlimited pressure on me to change my personality. My desires to get enough intellectual activity to feel alive were interpreted as arising from inflated ideas of my own importance which made me think I was different from other people. My vitality, under the combined influence of low intellectual input and brainwashing, diminished.

If you are frustrated in a way that it is not socially acceptable to understand, it is not merely that your problems are ignored, but that you find yourself with a whole new social identity, refuting which would apparently have to precede any statement of your actual problems, but which it is impossible to refute, although limitless quantities of energy could be expended on futile attempts to do so.

Supposing you suspect someone of running a drug ring; this is, in the nature of things, something that they can never disprove. If they were running one, it would be by definition concealed; so any display of sobriety or respectability can be dismissed as a front. So any consideration of one's situation as an exiled academic is removed to an enormous distance; it is postponed to that inaccessible future in which one will have proved to everyone's satisfaction that one is none of the things they want to think one is.

I found that this situation arose as soon as I was frustrated at school. As soon as I had been prevented from taking the School Certificate, I had problems. But also, apparently in response to this fact, I found myself being credited with problems I had not got at all, and having to argue about whether I had got them, apparently as a preliminary to any consideration of any problems I might think I had.

At first I thought that if you listened to all that people had to say, and answered as politely as possible, they would see that there was nothing in their suppositions, and then the way would be clear for me to say that I was being very badly affected by intellectual frustration.

So, when I was thirteen and fourteen, I was drawn into interminable discussions of myself and whether there was anything wrong with what I thought or didn't think about human relationships. But I found that these conversations, protracted though they were, never got anywhere near to anything that I considered a real point; and then I started to feel guilty at letting myself be drawn into them because they were a waste of time, and perhaps I should be able to solve my problems for myself by not wasting time and working as if things were different, without trying to make anyone understand anything or help me to arrange anything.

A lot of harm was done during the three years that elapsed before I was sixteen and could take some exams. Although I then got distinctions in all I took and won a State Scholarship straight away, I was actually all but un-functional.

I won the top scholarship to Somerville College a year or so later, but by now I was, really, in a horrific state.

It is no use trying to make a distinction between intellect and emotion. Real intellectual activity is a very emotional thing. I was very good at living intensely and at functioning at a high level of capacity. You couldn't demand, as had been demanded, that I live as if I were an un-intense, un-purposeful, undirected, half-hearted person without throwing my personality into a state of deadlock. Nevertheless, it was and is very effective for the sort of thing it is good at.

Everyone is only too intensely aware that the methods employed by the individual ego to defend itself may involve departures from realism. This awareness fails to be balanced by any corresponding awareness that methods of attack on the individual are not any more likely to be strictly objective.

In fact, the universal awareness of the tendency of an individual to desire to preserve some sort of acceptable self-image is itself a method of attack, since it can always be represented to him that any interpretation of the situation which is not horrendously destructive of his self-esteem is the flimsiest and gauziest of wishful thinking.

Perhaps the most characteristic use of this awareness that the individual psychology may seek to preserve a favourable self-image is in the prevention of any discussion of individual frustration. It is always acceptable to shift the discussion into a discussion of the individual's beliefs about himself in comparison with other people.

Thus, when I first arrived in Oxford I said to my tutor that I was very unhappy because I had never worked. (I knew this was rash, even at the time, but I was desperate.)

'But you've got the top scholarship,' she said. 'What more do you want?'

'I don't see that has anything to do with it,' I said. 'I haven't really been able to work for years, and I know I've never used my ability.'

'But you're just an ordinary person,' she said, quite rapidly.

So of course I gave up. Of course it was a corollary of what I had said that if I had actually used my ability in any way I regarded as using it, I would by that time have achieved an extraordinary amount. If you turned it into a question whether I was asserting that my abilities were extraordinary, of course discussion was impossible. It then became a question of self-image and it had to be right for everyone's self-image to think of themselves as more or less average, so you couldn't possibly

16

discuss what effects the underfunctioning of your abilities might have had.

Then again, consider the sort of response you are liable to get in adult life if you complain of being frustrated for lack of money. People are liable to tell you that Mozart was penniless, so you shouldn't mind; as if all that is in question is your vanity, which will certainly be salved by the consideration that various people of high ability in the past have found themselves unable to use it to extract an income from society. Any consideration of the conditions of life that you actually find necessary to well-being, or of the things that are not being done, is unnecessary.

I was, as has been explained, by now functioning at about the lowest ebb. Since I wasn't likely to receive any assistance in becoming functional again, I took to thinking about psychology.

My reflections on psychology were entirely original; you will find very little that resembles any of them in any known system. Eventually, as a side result, I worked out how to do ESP. My system of psychology was effectively complete by the time I was twenty-one.

All the time I was at college I went on trying to screw solutions to maths problems out of myself without any motivation at all. Actually there was some negative motivation; I really liked maths and I did not like doing it in horrific circumstances, which I felt was only spoiling it.

It was theoretical physics that I had been wanting to do all along. In spite of the overwhelmingly adverse circumstances, it was still possible that I might do well enough in the degree to get a research scholarship. When I went to the physics department to discuss it, I found the psychological outlook of all the physicists there so repellent that I knew I would not be able to get on with them or work there. (For some indication of my views on the psychology of the modern academic world in general, and the physicists in particular, see my book *The Decline and Fall of Science*.)

I knew that if I did not get a research scholarship to do theoretical physics I would have to found a research organisation for myself to do parapsychology and theoretical physics (the only two things I wanted to do, and I don't think of them as entirely separate).

This was a prospect which appalled me, as I knew I had no money, no contacts, and no social recognition.

However, I think perhaps that visit to the physics department was the last straw. I had been hoping to give myself an idea of a light at the end of the tunnel to motivate myself to work for the degree for the last few months. It had the reverse effect. There was a real sense in which I didn't want a research scholarship, even if the alternative was horrifying.

I worked as best one can with no motivation. They sort of changed the syllabus as well that year, so that my preparations, based on the previous years' papers, were ineffective. So, in the event, I got a Second, and no research scholarship, and got a job at the Society for Psychical Research (since I had no money) while I thought how to found my research organisation.

*

Havelock Ellis points out that educational success has not been very highly correlated with significant achievement in later life.[1] One of the reasons for this (as he points out) is that people later recognised as geniuses have strong tendencies to pursue autonomous lines of their own. This is a different matter from being able to interest oneself in whatever the educational system presents to one, at the age at which it sees fit to present it. Although there had been a time when I could think of nothing better than taking exams (being, of course, too young) before the end of my education I found it impossible to prevent my mind from pursuing lines of its own.

It seems to me that this is very likely to happen if no allowance is made for precocity; i.e. that with an extremely high I.Q. the optimum age for getting qualifications is likely to be earlier than if one has merely a high one.

[1] Havelock Ellis, *A Study of British Genius*, Hurst and Blackett, London, 1904.

In the University of Oxford there used to be more understanding than there is now of the fact that there were a lot of ways in which a person of very high ability could get disconnected from his education, but that this ability might still be too good to waste. T. E. Lawrence, as he approached his final examinations in history, regarded himself as unprepared for them; and it may be doubted whether he would have got a First if a tutor, sympathetic to his evident ability, had not drawn to his attention the possibility of offering a thesis on a subject of special interest to him to supplement the usual papers, and been instrumental in arranging finance for an expedition necessary for the proposed thesis.

There was always a certain tradition that colleges could, and sometimes did, if they knew a person had very high ability, disregard his examination results and make it possible for him to continue his academic career. When I was an undergraduate there was a story about a certain Professor who had got a Fourth, but had still gone on with his academic career and arrived at his present eminence. Even while I was at college a case occurred of a girl who got a Third, but the dons liked her and thought she was suited to doing research, so she duly got a research scholarship.

Of course, with the advance of socialism and the increased dependence of the colleges (or, strictly speaking, the university) on state finance, the tendency is for nothing to matter except exam results, regardless of how they have been brought about.

Even when there was some willingness to take ability into account and to make allowances for it, the safety net was, I am sure, far from a hundred per cent reliable. I knew an ex-Ambassador who, after being top scholar of his college (as I was of mine) was thrown out with a Third Class degree. In this case, so far as I can gather, this arose from his inability to produce the sort of philosophical views that were required at that time.

At the age of about seventy, when I knew him, he still remembered vividly the desolation of wandering the streets after being thrown out of his college, unable to continue the life he had intended as an academic and a poet. In fact, he was taken into the Foreign Office (which I think would be unlikely now; they too are much keener on First Class degrees as the only condition of entry). Having, in fact, high ability in spite of his lack of a good degree, once in the Foreign Office he rose to be an Ambassador.

In the modern ideology, again as I have experienced it in practice, it is apparently totally unacceptable for anyone of high ability to claim that there are reasons why they are not as functional as they would like to be. I did not see my being unable to do well enough in a maths degree as proving anything much about my ability, but only as the final outcome of a horrifically unhappy education.

The socially approved attitude was that it proved I should give up all idea of doing research in anything for all the rest of my life and turn myself into the sort of person who finds it possible to live outside of the academic world. Unable to adopt this attitude, I became the object of every sort of opprobrium and opposition (but the opposition wasn't all that much of a novelty).

When I left college, I thought, 'People may not support me because of the presumption that my education was a meaningful condemnation of me. After all, I might have been spending all those years in idleness, frivolity or depravity instead of struggling hopelessly with torments of frustration. And my aptitude for academic pursuits being so great, it is true that, if that were the explanation, a very high degree of idleness, frivolity or depravity would be necessary to account for my emerging without a single usable qualification. So if I get on with my academic career in the wilderness as best I can without support, surely the demonstration of quite a small amount of determination and industry will prove to people that it is necessary to consider some other explanation of my education going so tragically wrong and perhaps gradually they will start to take pity on me and give me financial support.'

I would not say that I ever pinned a great deal of faith to this, but it seemed to be the best hope there was. I still was not quite cynical enough to predict with confidence what would actually follow. Since a very high degree of idleness, frivolity and depravity would be necessary to justify my position as a social exile, I would come to be credited with just those things.

When I was thrown out at the end of my education Einstein got to be a much more significant figure in my scheme of things. He was the only person I knew about who had been rejected from the academic world and eventually taken back into it. Of course, even if one knew of no previous example, it would remain a theoretical possibility that such a thing could happen, but placed as one was, the concrete case became a thing to hang on to. The improbability of it seemed, at that time, heart-sinking, because it was only too easy to see it as the only chance that was at all easy to formulate of returning to a tolerable life.

It seems less emotionally loaded now, of course, because actually one has constructed a tolerable academic environment for oneself, albeit minimal and precarious.

But it seemed important then, and in a way still is, always to do one's work as if one believed that one day one would be accepted back, and to keep up the same standards as if one were having one's career inside the academic world instead of outside it.

That is only a matter of moralisation, not of probability, so it doesn't exactly affect the situation that it is now, in a sense, even harder to imagine how the University could possibly come to view me with any favour. But it is only that what one abstractly expected has become concrete. One always supposed that there would be no sympathy for an exiled academic struggling to get on with their career as best they could notwithstanding; now one knows of the specific kind and degree of hostility that has been evinced by specific people.

People's reactions to the case of Einstein (of which few are aware before being told) are interesting. Undergraduates are, typically, taken aback when they first realise that so successful a person was thrown out of the academic world. Then they brighten and say, 'But he was taken back and that proves that anybody good enough would always be taken back.' Then, very often, they say or imply that I ought to think all I have done since leaving college has been no good because if it had been I would have been given a Fellowship, or otherwise recognised.

Why do people have this desire to belive that society is an infallible arbiter of merit. I never had it; I thought anomalies and tragedies could happen, though I didn't have much of an opinion about how common they were.

*

There is a kind of psychology for crash-landing in a desert; you are shocked and adrenalised but there is no scope for emotional indulgence. There was once, I think, a film called *The Damned Don't Cry,* which about expresses it. If you crash-land you don't relieve your feelings by bursting into tears (at least, I rather imagine people don't), you start to progress in the direction you may find food, even if your legs are broken and you can only crawl. There is a practicality about it; you are trying to make your way back to a life in which the pleasure principle operates, meanwhile all that is in abeyance and what counts is crawling.

As I mentioned before, within a few months of leaving college I had taken a job at the Society for Psychical Research.

In the centre drawer of my desk at the office I kept graphs of my savings; also I had an account book. I regarded as automatic savings as high a proportion as I could of my pay; the rest I divided into daily increments, and then the object was, each day, to spend as little as possible so as to save some extra shillings out of the day's allocation.

One other way it was like a desert was that, as conditions were so unfavourable to life, you didn't know how far you could get before your energy gave out, and whether you would be able to reach better conditions before it was too late.

At first I tried to do physics every evening when I got back from the office, but I found it didn't work. I had the feeling of not having woken up all day because, at the office, there had been nothing to wake up for; so I went and walked around Kensington Gardens until I felt in a more normal state and able to start doing physics, but by then it was too late. So then I took to working late at the office in the evenings whenever I could, because at least for that I got a bit more pay. If the present was no good, I thought, it could at least buy the future.

By the end of the first year I had saved £300, which wasn't so bad out of a salary of £500. I felt a bit better then, because £300 had been my first target. Once I had it I could always, at a pinch, support myself for a year to do physics. I thought I would really want to feel free to pursue my thoughts for more than a year, and also I suspected I was going to found an organisation before I felt I could settle down, but at least there was the possibility.

About that time I met an influential socialist lady in her daughter's room in Somerville. 'Isn't it marvellous,' her daughter said, 'what a lot Celia's saved.' 'But whatever,' her mother said, pleased as a pussy-cat with her incomprehension, 'would she want to do that for. She must have lived on the edge of poverty. And it doesn't seem that she wants it for travel . . . or personal adornment . . .'

Well; she knew of course that my application for a research scholarship had been turned down, and that I was condemned to exclusion for life from the academic world. I don't see what else she could expect me to do.

By the same token that, when I was at school, I could be reduced to abject misery by not being able to work hard enough, I rated my chances of survival outside of the academic world as absolutely nil. There was nothing to be done but to create an academic world around myself, or at least to move in the direction of doing so. In this I was only following the law of the planecrash victim surrounded by desert. You stay by the plane if there is any hope of rescue, otherwise you walk in whatever direction is most likely to get you to food. Certainly I knew I couldn't depend on anyone to rescue me, so I started to walk.

I set up the legal constitution of a research institute and appealed for money. 'It's begging,' said the socialist lady, taunting. 'Well,' I thought. 'What do you expect? If that's what you call appealing directly to individuals to recognise your potentialities and needs. It's the only recourse I'm left with, having managed to emerge from my education without a usable qualification. That's what I'm condemned to, outside of the academic world, being a beggar all the rest of my life; I knew that long ago.'

But you couldn't say I hadn't done what I could to legitimise my position. I had established at least the legal possibility of being paid a salary for something I could do.

\*

The foundation of the Institute was multiply determined.

If I had been an academic it is very probable, in fact virtually certain, that I would have thought of founding an organisation to do the research in parapsychology which I saw to be done; certainly I would never have gone through life like so many Oxford and Cambridge professors, saying that the best thing I could do for the subject was not to do it, but to collect as much social prestige as possible. (The point of this is, allegedly, that the prestige eventually rubs off on the subject.)

But as it was, as a ruined academic, I was obliged to construct an academic organisation around myself, by the same necessity that a shipwrecked sailor looks for food and constructs a shelter against the weather. If there had been no such thing as parapsychology, I would have founded an organisation to do theoretical physics, philosophy and psychology. That would have sounded a trifle odd, seeing that organisations already existed to do those things, but I would have done it nonetheless. As it was, the fact that parapsychology was not otherwise provided for gave my organisation a rationalised *raison d'être*, but made it no easier to finance. If I had founded an organisation to do physics it might have sounded unnecessary, but it would probably have found it no more difficult to raise funds. (A thing can't be more difficult than impossible.)

Even as it is, the terms of reference of this Institute actually do not restrict it to parapsychology. I took care, when the Trust Deed was being drawn up, that they were wide enough to include theoretical physics, etc., as well.

And this partly explains why I would not let it be called anything that included the word 'parapsychology'. Quite apart from not liking the implications of the word, even in relation to the areas of research to which it refers, I wouldn't have the Institute's interests restricted in that way.

Viewed as the driftwood shelter of a shipwrecked academic, this Institute is not so bad, penniless though it is.

*

## Advice to Clever Children

Think hard about the motivation of those who have power over you. They are not going to understand you; you had better understand them.

They may tell you that people often blame the environment for difficulties caused by their own weaknesses. Beware. Why are they motivated to cover up for the environment?

They may tell you that intellectual achievement is not everything in life. Ask yourself: what *else* is there?

# An Invitation to Young People

As may already have become apparent from the Introduction to this book, we are endeavouring to build up a sort of private sector university, or at least a college *cum* research department, here in Oxford. The essential ingredients in constructing such a thing are people and money.

If you think there is any possibility that you might be interested in joining forces with us, please write. It is usually desirable for people to come and live near us in Oxford, supporting themselves in the first instance, while they get to know more about us, and we find out what they are best adapted to doing.

An interest in the phenomena stigmatised as paranormal is not enormously relevant; in fact, if such an interest is in any way associated with a particular world-view, or if you regard paranormal phenomena as supporting any particular beliefs, it is unlikely that you would find working with us congenial for long. Some degree of liking for my general outlook, as expressed in the present book and in my two earlier books *The Human Evasion* and *The Decline and Fall of Science,* is however probably necessary.

A particularly high I.Q. or a strong aptitude for academic pursuits is unnecessary. If you find our outlook at all congenial, and the prospect of working with us attractive, there are sure to be plenty of things that you can do.

On the other hand, we are primarily an organisation for the purpose of research, and people of the highest intellectual ability will find that there is plenty of scope for it to be used if they join us.

# An Appeal for Financial Support

I know it is hardly the socially done thing to claim to be an unrecognised genius and a charming modesty is supposed to be a desirable attribute. However, this is easier if you have a compatible position in society which allows you some scope for doing things. Having been, from the age of thirteen, forced into a position of exile from my natural position in society, I am obliged to insist on the discrepancy between my potentialities and anything I am able to do in practice. I have, after all, spent the last twenty years trying to work towards a position in which I could implement some of my ideas for research, but I can't say that patient merit is a particularly good method of getting reward or recognition.

In stressing the wastage of my own abilities, I do not mean to underestimate the potentialities of the other members of the Institute staff. In fact, the prevailing level of I.Q. is extremely high, and I much regret that the others also are obliged to spend so much of their time merely surviving. However, I think it is better to present the case primarily in terms of an exceptional individual. One is then arguing on a more realistic footing, and gets away from this unrealistic idea of any organisation mechanically carrying out prescribed projects. The fact is that if I have any freedom of operation at all, I am incapable of not finding out things never known before. Fortunately or unfortunately I have a flair for appreciating the points of real and far-reaching theoretical significance. I am also sufficiently aware of the operative areas of psychology to know that most people necessarily have emotional resistances to perceiving exactly this. However, if given any freedom to operate I am sure I could make the modern scientific establishment extremely uncomfortable.

While it may be that a millionaire, or even a multi-millionaire, is necessary to establish a research organisation on a realistic scale, I would not be inclined to despise the assistance which might be given by anyone who felt tolerably adapted to their role in society and was earning a normal salary for it. If all of such people to whom I have ever explained my terrible position were to have contributed a tenth of their salary, I should be by now in rather a good position to make use of my abilities.

# Aphorisms

I write this book in the confident expectation that it will be misunderstood.

*

To think that there are no people at all in the world makes it feel empty: this explains the otherwise puzzling fact that people go on being taken in by one another.

*

You can never possess anything finite; that only leaves the infinite.

*

The only hope for the most of the human race is despair.

*

Has your transcendental majesty time to consider its happiness? Who was it said: I leave living to the servants? For my part, I will leave happiness to slaves.

*

Young people wonder how the adult world can be so boring. The secret is that it is not boring to adults because they have learnt to enjoy simple things like covert malice at one another's expense. This is why they talk so much about the value of human understanding and sympathy. It has a certain rarity value in their world.

*

How immoderately moderate are the highest aspirations of the human race!

*

The perception of the unreality of reality is the beginning of psychological realism.

*

There is nothing so risky as security.

*

The despair of urgency and the despair of significance and the despair of being itself.

*

*'We're all in the same boat, you know. You're no worse off than anyone else.'*
The sequence of ideas from 'many people are in a bad situation' to 'no one should mind about the bad situation' does not bear analysis – intellectual analysis, that is. But it is perfectly comprehensible as a statement of an emotional position.

*

There are two ways of living, one of which leads to astonishment and the other to boredom.

*

There are two possible kinds of psychology. It is evident that both are possible since it is only necessary for one person to have each kind of psychology to establish its possibility. One of them is possible to me; the other is evidently possible to nearly everybody else.

*

Children need admiration rather than affection.

*

One should not underestimate the speed of maturation of humans; most children soon learn how to degrade one another by reference to social standards; anyone who does this is really an adult.

*

Progress towards sanity is achieved by abandoning first the desire for omnipotence and then that for exceptional achievement.

*

It was one of the paradoxes of my education that the unhurried timescale on which it was conducted resulted ultimately in states of mind in which there was no time to think, whereas working 'too hard' and doing things unreasonably fast resulted (on the few occasions I got away with it) in an enormously spacious lucidity in which everything was clear and simple and there was all the time in the world.

*

The difference between learning fast and learning slowly is not that the same mental processes happen, only faster or slower as the case may be. Either you are learning fast enough for mental processes to happen, or they do not happen at all.

*

The human race wished me to accept the limitations with which it had thoughtfully provided me.

*

There is a strange concern for purity of motivation, which the human race shows in no other context than that of discrediting aspiration. (You shouldn't actually want to *succeed* — just love your work for itself . . .)

*

The phrase 'real life' may almost infallibly be taken to mean 'the most repetitive elements of human life' or 'that which human lives have in common with a considerable section of the animal kingdom'. So in this phrase the concept 'reality' is seen to be a kind of compound of 'physiological processes' and 'monotony'.

*

*'Life at a university with its intellectual and inconclusive discussions is, on the whole, a bad training for the real world and only men with a very strong character surmount this handicap.'* (Sir Paul Chambers, Chairman of ICI, Chuter Ede Lecture, 1964.)

The phrase 'real life' is often used to mean 'everything which can be relied upon to distract and disillusion any young person who still has hopes, ideals and ambitions'.

*

The human race is so extremely ungreedy.

*

Sane people regard meanness as a sort of religion.

*

A normal life-cycle is one in which you give up your hope of anything ever happening.

*

Geniuses want to be frustrated, so one should let them be; unless they do not want to be frustrated, in which case they are what is called 'unbalanced', and one should certainly not help them then, on account of their moral turpitude.

*

Success has lost its meaning for sane people. What they mean by success is destroying other people.

*

The one thing people are unconditional about is putting other people in the wrong. They will deprive themselves of everything they want rather than miss the opportunity of doing this.

*

It is supposed that self-sacrifice is the prerogative of altruism. On the contrary; the sacrifices of sadism are the greater.

*

The desire for exceptional achievement is no longer of central importance to the mature person. Even if the opportunity for such achievement were offered him, he would regard it as only secondary to his interest in ensuring that other people cannot achieve anything either.

*

*Love* (in modern sociology, etc.) means 'to interact continuously and absorbingly with other people in such a way as to keep everyone's mind off reality, but without actually killing them'.

*

Humanity says, 'I am a jealous god. Thou shalt have no other gods before me.'

*

'Love your neighbour as yourself.' – 'Love that in your neighbour which resembles you.' – 'Love those who do not surpass you.'

*

*On belief in survival after death:*
It doesn't matter at all what you do with your life while you are waiting to survive.

*

*An example of sane logic* – you must take the rough with the smooth. (Bad for analytical thought.)

*

'Thou shalt not think about the universe; and thou shalt hate thy neighbour as thyself.'

*

The normal personality consists of its right to deny rational communication.

*

If you are analytical you find out about reality, so sane people prefer not to be.

*

I think people talk so much about the importance of 'exchanging ideas' because it is actually impossible in their world. Everyone has so dense a layer of reactive personality that to talk objectively about anything is out of the question.

*

I would be sorry for everyone living on the ordinary terms, if they showed any sign of knowing how to be sorry for themselves.

*

People might die as if they meant it.

*

I would rather regard myself as a failure than anything as impossible.

*

The psychology of sane people is always worse rather than better than one might imagine.

*

In the universe there is room for an infinite series of beginnings.

CHAPTER 1

# Inconceivability

The perception that existence exists invalidates the normal personality, as does the imminence of death. (I am aware that there are various examples of people preserving their normal interests on their death-beds, or on the eve of execution; the question is whether they ever actually *perceived* the imminence of death.)

I must insist on the word 'perception'; it is not a matter of using the verb 'to be' freely and efficiently. I think you may be said to have the relevant perception when you see that it is inconceivable that anything should exist; or perhaps simply that it is *astonishing* that anything should be there at all. The latter is perhaps the less analytical.

Now if you see that it is inconceivable that anything should exist, it is evident that at least one inconceivable fact is there; that is to say, that which exists is not limited to the conceivable.

Since the inconceivable *is there*, it is impossible to set any limit to the quantity of inconceivableness which may be present in the situation.

Now were the existence of anything consistently to remind you of the fact of inconceivability, since it is impossible to live without interacting with a large number of existing things, it would be impossible for you to feel in the same way about the conceivable. However, on the contrary, most people feel that this very interaction with existing things justifies them in taking into account only things that they can think about.

Actually the fact that *the inconceivable exists* sheds a certain doubt on any conceivable association of ideas, because there may always be more facts (of an inconceivable kind) which are, *in reality,* relevant.

35

Now if anyone were reminded of the inconceivable by the fact of existence at all constantly, he would sooner or later have the perception that there may be inconceivable considerations which are inconceivably more important than any conceivable consideration could be. I do not think it is possible to have a *perception* that the conceivable is of necessity far more important than the inconceivable, although it is certainly possible to live in such a way that all one's emotional attitudes are consistent with this assumption. (This is the almost universal condition of man.)

Now if you do have a perception that any conceivable consideration may be utterly invalidated by some other consideration which you do not know, and if you are reminded of this perception constantly by the fact that things exist, certain modifications take place in the way you feel about things. These modifications have not taken place in the psychology of most people.

For example, you would not be able to think 'Our happiness is here or not at all' without also thinking 'There may be important and inconceivable facts in relation to which it does not matter at all whether we are happy or not; it may even be the case that for some quite inconceivable reason it is much the best thing that I should be as unhappy as possible.'[1]

I return therefore to my initial statement: The perception that existence exists invalidates the normal personality.

*

Since the fact of existence is inconceivable there *may* be an

[1] The dictum, 'Our happiness is here or not at all', was once quoted to me as supporting an outlook on life somewhat different from my own. I believe it is derived from the following lines of Wordsworth:

> 'Not in Utopia, — subterranean fields, —
> Or some secreted island, Heaven knows where!
> But in the very world, which is the world
> Of all of us, — the place where, in the end,
> We find our happiness, or not at all!'
>                     The Prelude, XI, 140.

unlimited quantity of inconceivability. Perhaps you do not think the fact of existence *is* inconceivable; well, set it against its opposite, non-existence: no space, no time, no anything at all. Is that conceivable? Now what makes existence what it is is what distinguishes it from non-existence, and this is inconceivable.

But enough. It cannot, I grant, be demonstrated. In the last resort you *perceive* it, or you do not. I do not even claim that it is an easy perception to have, though an obvious one. It is an open secret, as Carlyle – following Goethe – said (though perhaps he was not referring to the identical perception); but the operative word is 'secret'.

Now I think it is fairly obvious that any one inconceivable event or relationship is sufficient to establish that no limit can be set to the extent of the inconceivable. It is only possible to delimit relationships within defined and conceivable conceptual systems. You can say 'no two single-digit numbers can *possibly* add up to more than 18'. But you cannot place an inconceivable fact within the framework of a defined system of relationships, and consequently you have no way of delimiting or categorising the relationships which it may have.

So: an inconceivable fact *may* have inconceivable implications. (I do not ask you to accept that it *must* have, which again is a matter of perception, but I think an all but indisputable one; since if an inconceivable fact did not have inconceivable implications, this would itself be an outrageously inconceivable state of affairs.)

37

# CHAPTER 2

# Uncertainty

Philosophy is about reality (not common sense), and so long as it confines itself to stating that no limits can be set to possibility, it actually provides quite a useful guide to reality. All men of common sense would, I feel sure, think that things move away from you *because* you push them. But that 'because' has no force whatsoever. To call a push a 'force' and to assert that a 'force' is something which makes matter accelerate in the direction of the force, tells you, if you observe it closely, nothing at all.

Now modern physics has discovered that certain 'antiparticles' move in the opposite direction to the force. This, of course, merely makes explicit the gulf of uncertainty that always lay beneath that smooth bridge of familiarity from 'cause' to 'effect'. A human physicist, seeking to restore familiarity to the situation somehow, has named the new particle the 'donkey particle' – it moves towards you when you push, and away when you pull.

The degree of compatibility which a given idea has with the human mind, or the number of human beings prepared to accept it as a possibility, has no relevance whatever in assessing whether the idea is likely to be true, except that (if you are at all interested in reality) it would seem desirable to acquire the habit of discounting your emotional preferences – and everyone else's.

I decided at around the age of eleven that the fact of *uncertainty* was the last word in all questions. It appeared to me that to adopt any attitude which obscured one's awareness of this was unrealistic, and it appeared to me also that it established quite definite criteria about what were and were not realistic attitudes. E.g. I should have taken a very dim view of any half-explicit tendency to believe that the common sense opinions of the human race were anything to be relied upon. (Though I think I was never much tempted by that one.)

Applying this to survival after death, for example; in view of the total uncertainty, there can never be rigorous proof of survival in any form nor, indeed, that your annihilation will not occur one second from now (and the annihilation of all that exists, come to that). So, if one is interested in anything one might feel urgent about doing it without delay. Whatever one wants, one had better try and get it here and now, but personally I never thought happiness sounded interesting. (I am, of course, thinking again of that quotation, 'Our happiness is here or not at all'.)

*

The only irrefutable pieces of philosophy are those which assert that nothing is certain. I do not *assert* that there are no other people in the world, but I do assert that there is no way whatever of arriving at even a probabilistic weighting of the alternative propositions: 'Mine is the only consciousness; everything else is my dream', and 'All bodies that seem to behave more or less as I do have consciousnesses like mine'. If, therefore, one of these propositions appears in any way more probable than the other, this is the result of an emotional bias of a kind which is unreliable in all matters of scientific enquiry. It used to be found emotionally satisfactory to suppose, for example, that the sun went round the earth.

*

I do not use the word consciousness in a particularly abnormal sense; however, I do use it, and am prepared to classify various qualitatively different kinds of it. The first classification is between astonishment and the lack of it. It is a philosophical fact that we might reasonably experience emotions of astonishment and uncertainty at the position in which we find ourselves. It is a psychological fact (which must be established indepen-

39

dently, and cannot be inferred from the philosophical statement) that a state of consciousness characterised by astonishment at the fact of existence is possible. This state is also characterised by the fact that it is compatible with vivid perception of all philosophical statements of an irrefutable variety. The normal, or un-astonished state of consciousness is characterised by emotional indifference towards all irrefutable philosophical statements.

This may be seen as a symptom of its indifference to facts. Or, rather, its hatred of them; for reality, like pain, is too noticeable a phenomenon for mere diversion of attention to eliminate the conflicts caused by its presence. It follows that normal psychology is characterised by indifference to reality and by hatred of other people. (The hostility aroused by reality has to be displaced onto something.)

*

When I talk about 'seeing existence' I mean something quite precise by this. I mean the astonishment that anything should be existing at all. It is very closely related to the awareness of the total uncertainty. Perhaps one should say it is identical with it, though in incomplete forms it may be appropriate to describe the perception in one of these two ways rather than the other.

Normally, people only 'see existence' in flashes, but this is the result of the prevailing quality of their emotions – or of the motivation on which they are operating, which comes to the same thing.

To 'see existence' may be terrifying or liberating; both qualities follow from the fact that it is absolutely incompatible with normal attitudes. It simply invalidates the attempt to pretend that there is a closed system of *familiarities* within which you can operate meaningfully.

I use the adjective 'existential' to refer to emotions, attitudes, etc., of a kind which are compatible with a state in which one is 'seeing existence', whether or not they occur during it.

*

People sometimes seem to think that because I am in some ways critical of what is done in the modern world under the name of science, I must be wishing to reject scientific method or to say that the facts with which, for example, physics and biology deal are not 'real', and that we should be concerning ourselves with some other kind of reality altogether. Actually what I have against modern science is that it is applied selectively, and the results are interpreted tendentiously. I.e. only pieces of research which will seem to provide support for the prevailing ideology are likely to be done, and any results obtained are likely to be interpreted as proving far more than they actually do.

I do not think the facts described by physics and biology are not *real*, but I do not think it is *realistic* to consider them without remembering (a) that there is an indefinite quantity of equally *real* facts which we do not know, and (b) that so-called 'causal' relationships are matters of uncertainty, as Hume has demonstrated.

In particular, I regard physics as in some ways the supreme demonstration that the inconceivable exists. Physics is about reality; its mathematical clarity permits one to entertain not the slightest suspicion that the relationships being described are conceivable ones. (Of course, you may avert your eyes, mumbling 'it's only a mathematical convenience'. This is what most physicists do. Consequently physicists stay sane and physics advances slowly.)

And I have nothing against biology except that it is descriptive rather than analytical, and does not *prove things* in the way it is supposed to do. No amount of study of the life-cycle of the great-tit would succeed in convincing me that I ought to adopt certain attitudes and not others; the same applies to rats, monkeys and human beings.

# CHAPTER 3

# Guilt

I referred in the last chapter to the hostility with which human beings regard one another; a hostility which is, in fact, a displaced form of aggression against the universe, and which is rationalised as altruism. 'The desire to punish arises when the source of authority, which is the natural object of aggression, is too powerful to be safely attacked.' Orthodox psycho-analysis will go so far. But it is not, of course, prepared to extend its findings to include reactions to the human situation as such. By extension, it transpires that everyone wants to punish everyone else, and this is, on inspection, seen to explain the facts of human interaction quite adequately.

Illustration: A few days ago a farm labourer was reported drowned in a ditch under an overturned combine harvester. No one wrote to *The Times* saying: 'The human situation cannot go on.' On the contrary, there is a noticeable demand for news items of this type, so they evidently appeal to something in human psychology.

(The Sleeper turns in his uneasy sleep under the Tree Yggdrasil. He mutters: 'Who shall deliver me from the body of this death?' but does not wake.)

*

However, what I am really trying to write about is the existential criterion, and how one can distinguish between that order of psychology which is compatible with existential perceptions, and that which is not.

Hostility is not a very good thing to start with, if the object is to shed light on how the criterion works. The perception that existence is astonishing provides no direct reason why you should or should not feel anything in particular about other people. What it does provide is an invalidation of anthropocentric and sociocentric emotions – of all kinds. It is not possible to perceive the total uncertainty and to enter into a social situation: a fact which has been observed by philosophers (e.g. Hume) and made use of – to dispel perceptions of total uncertainty.

One may also observe – though perhaps this is a subtle observation which one is not likely to make until the existential criterion has become dominant in one's thinking – that it is *particularly* difficult to entertain any emotion depending on (or containing any concealed element of dependence on) social justification. 'Society would agree that you have wronged me, so I am justified in feeling resentment' is unthinkable; but so is 'Society would agree that I should feel altruistic emotions in this situation, so I am justified in feeling them.'

This is, after all, what you would expect when you consider that the existential perception invalidates all forms of security; any emotion, therefore, that depends on an unquestionable standard (however implicit) is untenable.

Now consider how the existential criterion applies to guilt. It is obviously impossible to feel guilt in view of the total uncertainty. You do not know what anything is about; how then can you feel guilt? Guilt is plainly an entirely social emotion which depends on assumed standards; not to mention fear of other humans, hatred of them, and fear that they may discover your hatred.

The existential analogue of guilt is the fear of finiteness, or cosmic claustrophobia. It is not, psycho-dynamically, a precise analogue; but the two things are plainly related by being ways in which one might experience anxiety at being what one is, and the closeness of the psychological relation is shown by the fact that a discussion of guilt is regularly substituted in all contexts where a discussion of finiteness might seem in order.

Religion, for example, has commonly assumed that it was concerned primarily with the problem of sin and guilt, and only indirectly with that of finiteness. If it refers to the latter at all, it is with the implication that it is sinful and presumptuous to

43

mind about it. (The object of religion being to reconcile us to our creaturely condition, of course – or to our social environment.)

Sometimes the two things are discussed in parallel – e.g. by Tillich, who will talk of 'the anxiety of naked existence' and 'the anxiety of personal guilt'. It is illuminating that he does not suggest that guilt is invalidated by the perception of naked existence; if anything, he implies that 'personal guilt' is the more fundamental anxiety. However, he recognises the potency of the existential perception in asserting, 'It is impossible for a finite being to stand naked anxiety for more than a flash of time.'[1] Observe the categorical and sweeping nature of this statement. Not 'I do not know of anyone who . . . .' or 'Probably no human being . . .'; but 'It is impossible for a finite being . . .'. (Of all the orders of intellect, incarnate or discarnate, which may exist in this universe, I am utterly *certain* that not one could think about reality for more than an infinitesimal instant of time.)

This confidence is, of course, completely unrealistic in the sense that it can have no philosophical justification. The total uncertainty does not permit you to infer from your past states of mind that states of mind radically different are not possible. Even if it could be proved that no human being had ever considered reality for more than a flash of time, this would still not constitute a proof that no human being ever could do so.

But, of course, a statement like Tillich's is to be understood as a description of a psychological state. It means, 'I am completely unaware of the total uncertainty most of the time; when I am aware of it it gives me a shock; fortunately to be unaware of it is socially accepted as a justified and virtuous state.' Or, even more simply, 'I do not want to be aware of the total uncertainty.'

Incidentally, all recognised forms of bonkersdom are admitted to operate on things like the guilt syndrome indicated above (hostility – concealment – fear, etc.). I am driven to the word

[1] Paul Tillich, *The Courage to Be*, Collins Fontana Books, London, 1952, p. 47.

'bonkersdom' since 'madness' has become unfashionable and the tendentious expression 'mental illness' implies that the unrecognised forms of bonkersdom should rightfully be described as 'mental health'.

*

C. S. Lewis in *Perelandra* has an idea about the Fall of man depending on the rejection of insecurity. Well: paraphrase a little. When you see a ball falling, do you accept the insecurity of the (philosophically irrefutable) fact that you have no way of knowing what it will do next? Or do you confidently wait for it to reach the ground?

# CHAPTER 4

# Suffering

In religious books we find that the intolerableness of being finite is only recognised in the form of 'suffering by a child'. In terms of sane psychology there is a good reason for this. Children are not yet so good at dishonesty as adults, and they may therefore experience reality more or less as it is; that is, for one thing, as intolerable (when experienced on the usual terms). For this reason, of course, the adult world has a vested interest in supposing them to be intrinsically inferior, and to need protection from reality at any cost.

Now personally I would be prepared to regard a moment of suffering by any consciousness as invalidating the whole range of pleasures possible in life. It may make some difference to the quality of the suffering whether the consciousness is in a state of more or less profound dishonesty, but it makes no difference to the absoluteness of the phenomenon.

However, when this phenomenon is discussed in this kind of book, it never seems to lead to the conclusion that pleasure is rendered invalid. Nor, indeed, does it lead to the conclusion that we should be reminded of the fact that the purpose of the universe may have nothing whatever to do with us.

The consideration of the problem seems to involve us only in a choice between two possibilities which are certainly not logically exclusive.[1] These possibilities are, on the one hand, that there is a God who is deeply concerned about the preservation of human comfort, and on other hand, that there is no God at all — that is to say, that the Universe is a phenomenon which derives from no cause whatsoever.

---

[1] I.e. the only two alternatives considered certainly do not exhaust the possible formulations of possible states of affairs that might be enunciated.

46

The interesting thing to be observed is that these writers are prepared to ask whether we should give up our faith in God (whatever that means). They are never prepared to ask whether we should give up our faith in the situation in which we find ourselves. They go through contortions of dishonesty; first, in pretending that they are unbearably harrowed by the sufferings of children; and secondly, in pretending that it costs them great efforts to 'accept' these sufferings.

> In this sermon, Paneloux declared that nothing was more important than a child's suffering, and that there were no answers to such a problem. We have our backs against the wall, and there are no simple devices by which that wall can be scaled. He refused to claim that the child's suffering would be matched by an eternity of bliss; besides, who could say that even endless bliss could compensate for a moment of suffering here? . . . The suffering of a child could not be reconciled to anything we know about God. It forced us to the wall, without an answer. But, he asked, do we dare to give up our faith in God because of this? Rieux would answer, 'Yes, we must.' . . . This is no answer to a child's suffering, but a recognition that we must live with such injustice as our normal lot in this life.[1]

Applying the existential criterion: what reactions to suffering are compatible with the existential perception? Well, in the first place, not dishonest ones. I think it is not making too technical a point to say that an interest in existence (i.e. that which is there) cannot co-exist with a disinterest in facts; I include psychological facts.

Now it is a psychological fact that most people, confronted with the possibility of death by plague, would find the prospect of their own suffering more directly disturbing than that of any child's or adult's. It is merely being socially acceptable to pretend that the most harrowing thing in the situation is not your own suffering, but a child's.

Incidentally, any very young child would know quite clearly that he was most afraid of catching the plague himself. (Of such is the Kingdom of Heaven.)

[1] From discussion of Camus's *Plague* in William Hamilton, *The New Essence of Christianity*, Darton, Longman and Todd, London, 1966, pp. 50–1.

Now the most childish reaction to this situation is also the most philosophically justifiable; because you do not know whether anyone else has a consciousness or not; but you do know about your own.

So, to be honest, we should discuss our own sufferings. If you do perceive (and it is not a common perception) that an eternity of bliss is invalidated by a moment's suffering, then you must also admit that a life-time's pleasure is.

It is quite dishonest to claim to see the more extreme thing without allowing it to have any effect on your life. Now in fact, the existential[1] reaction to suffering is that it invalidates everything except the most intense and directed way of living. This is not logically justifiable, but psychologically. There is an enemy; what shall I do? Fight or flight; attack or run hard. Not sit down peaceably and enjoy the view. It is therefore a psychological law that if you see finiteness is intolerable, you can no longer do things which are not sufficiently intense to constitute a reaction to what you have seen.

\*

Some quotations from Tillich, with comments.

> The walls of distance, in time and space, have been removed by technical progress; but the walls of estrangement between heart and heart have been incredibly strengthened . . . But let us just consider ourselves and what we feel, when we read, this morning and tonight, that in some sections of Europe all children under the age of three are sick and dying, or that in some sections of Asia millions without homes are freezing and starving to death. The strangeness of life to life is evident in the strange fact that we can know all this, and yet can live today, this morning, tonight, as though we were completely ignorant. And I refer to the most sensitive people among us. In both mankind and nature, life is separated from life. Estrangement prevails among all things that live. Sin abounds.[2]

If you think you should be harrowed by the thought of the starving millions, why should you not be harrowed by your own

[1] I habitually use the word 'existential' in my own sense; no compatibility with the attitudes of 'existentialist' writers such as Camus is implied.

[1] Paul Tillich, *The Shaking of the Foundations*, Penguin Books, London, 1962, pp. 159–60.

48

position of vulnerability to pain and annihilation? But in fact you are not disturbed by the latter; your indifference to the former follows incidentally but inevitably.

> It strikes us when we feel that our separation is deeper than usual, because we have violated another life, a life which we loved, or from which we were estranged. It strikes us when our disgust for our own being, our indifference, our weakness, our hostility, and our lack of direction and composure have become intolerable to us . . . Sometimes at that moment a wave of light breaks into our darkness, and it is as though a voice were saying: 'You are accepted. *You are accepted,* accepted by that which is greater than you, and the name of which you do not know. Do not ask for the name now; perhaps you will find it later. Do not try to do anything now; perhaps later you will do much. Do not seek for anything; do not perform anything; do not intend anything. *Simply accept the fact that you are accepted!*'[1]

It is never permitted to be very worried about our own finiteness; however, we are permitted to take fairly seriously the discrepancy between our actual and pretended motivation. But we must not take even this seriously for very long (or we might have some realistic thoughts about how pointless it is to keep pretending we 'care' about people, when we don't). This is where 'acceptance' comes in.

One must admire the ingenuity of the human race in turning religion into a positive aid to dishonesty.

I met someone the other day who said he understood what Dr. John Robinson meant when he said God was something you found deep down in human relationships.[2] God is the ultimate dishonesty?

> This is the situation of all men. But not all men know it. 'Yet who knoweth the power of thine anger, and who of us dreads thy wrath? So teach us to count our days, that we may get a heart of wisdom!' The 90th Psalm tries to teach us the truth about our human situation, our transitoriness and our guilt. It does what the great ancient tragedies did . . . they showed the people that the greatest, the best, the most beautiful, the most powerful – all – stand under the tragic law and the curse of the immortals. They wanted to reveal the tragic situation of man, that is, his situation

[1] Ibid., pp. 163–4.
[2] Cf. John A. T. Robinson, *Honest to God*, S.C.M. Paperback, 1963.

before the Divine. He becomes great and proud and tries to touch the Divine sphere, and he is cast into destruction and despair.[1]

I might say, on the other hand, that the mediocre and non-aspiring are very particularly under the wrath of God. I can even give the statement a precise meaning, which is more than Tillich gives his. I shall define 'the wrath of God' to mean 'all those aspects of reality the awareness of which is incompatible with the present state of your psychology'. The non-aspiring man does not even notice that there are any aspects of reality which are incompatible with his psychological position; his unrealism is therefore the more profound.

[1] Tillich, op. cit., pp. 78–9.

# CHAPTER 5

# The Taboo on Thinking

The other day I was listening to some human beings talking. (It was at a university society meeting and they were ostensibly talking about what one might do with one's life.) There can be little doubt that the human race is mad.

It may be said that the defining characteristic of a psychotic utterance is that it is not meaningful except in relation to the psychological state which gives rise to it. Given enough information about the past experiences of a schizophrenic, you may come to understand what emotional attitude he is expressing when he says: 'Look! Look! The wheels up there!' But you need not be surprised that you cannot see the wheels.

The only thing that prevents the meaninglessness of most human utterances from being detected is that everyone has the same psychosis. It is not even necessary to know a person's past experience in detail; it is enough to know that he stands in a certain relation to the fact of existence — that of ignoring it.

Now the other night there was present a Jungian Christian (at least, so I inferred from his reactions) who started at a certain point to talk complete gibberish. As a result of considerable experience of this type of mental case, I recognised what he was saying to mean: 'Aren't we being a good deal too clear about this? Mustn't we leave ourselves room for dishonesty?' – he called it 'paradox'. But I can no more reproduce his precise (and very long) sequence of undefined terms and *non sequiturs* than I can reproduce the curious non-logic of the schizophrenic.

It included, of course, the habitual confusion which is always encountered in psychotics of this type between 'detachment' in the sense of 'disembodied existence' and in the sense of 'a decrease of emotional investment in the everyday concerns of the human race'. Persons of this type appear to think in terms of a very crude dichotomy between 'involvement, activity, intense interest in the affairs of the human race' on the one hand, and 'disembodied existence, stasis, lack of interest in the affairs of the human race' on the other. It is clear that their emotional disturbances in this area are such as to set up an all but insuperable resistance to the ideas of 'intense interest in something other than the affairs of the human race', or 'life in a physical body combined with disinterest in the physical world'.

As they are only concerned with supporting one another's psychotic condition, this leads to conversations about religion being conducted in a kind of symbolic shorthand, designed to remind them repeatedly of the simple dichotomy between 'everyday living' and 'stasis'.

'Oh well, you have to live in the world.'

'Some people withdraw, of course.'

'Oh well, not everyone can go and sit in a cell on the top of a mountain.'

'No, you have to get on with things.' – and so on.

Now the extraordinary thing is that even highly trained intellectuals are content to talk about this kind of thing in this kind of meaningless formula. For example, the word 'withdraw' could mean several different things, and the sentence containing it is a blank cheque until you have said which one of them you mean. You might mean 'physically' or 'emotionally' or 'physically and emotionally' – for example. But the group-psychosis depends on everyone accepting the same association of ideas in the crucial areas, and analytical discussion of these ideas is therefore *taboo*.

This is, of course, a far more profound taboo than the sex one, which has always been heavily signposted. This one is implicitly understood, and never needs to be referred to.

In actual fact, sex is entirely compatible with the human psychosis. Either you set a rigid taboo on it, so everyone can have a lot of interesting conflicts about not having it, or else you remove the taboo and everyone spends their time having it. I suppose the resistance to the abandonment of the taboo arose from the fact that people were afraid that if it were removed sex might become less interesting and the time spent on it might be reduced. But this fear was unfounded.

My analysis of the situation is, of course, based on the assumption that the true aim of human psychology is to keep human interaction at a maximum and thought about reality at a minimum.

Incidentally, what the human race remembers of the observations of Freud is both tendentious and selective.

It is tendentious in the sense that no amount of demonstration of the role played by sex in human interactions relieves you of the necessity of making a quite independent value judgement about the relative importance of sex in your scheme of things. If you evaluate sex as trivial, Freud may merely have shown that more human reactions were trivial than had formerly been supposed.

And as an example of selectivity in reading Freud, no one seems to have noticed his observation that expressions of sympathy, grief, etc., depend on the extent to which one possesses repressed feelings of hostility towards the suffering or deceased person. I arrived at this conclusion independently, by a quite different route; but in fact it is enough to listen to the gloat in people's voices: 'Oh, that is a *nasty* operation she's having.'

The human race has been having a public gloat recently about a mining disaster. 'Tragedy,' they say; 'Heart-rending,' they say; 'Turn to page 7 for the faces of the bereaved *in pictures*,' they say.

Do you seriously believe that anyone minds other people being crushed to death? If they did they would do something commensurate, not wallow in emotion.

Necessity is the mother of invention; the human race is under no necessity to change the human situation, consequently it hasn't the ghost of an idea how one might set about it.

# CHAPTER 6

# The Human Psychosis

The human psychosis is extremely simple. Hatred of reality (originally caused, it is to be supposed, by a traumatic experience or experiences of objective impotence) has become displaced on to other human beings. This state of affairs is expressed by attitudes of indifference to reality and of interest in human society. The latter interest is usually rationalised as altruism.

\*

The other day I was talking to a human being. I said: 'No one is interested in reality.' He said, 'Well, reality, what's that? Nothing exciting. That chair, this carpet.' 'There is the universe out there,' I said. 'Well, what's the universe?' he said. 'Some stars. Some of them we know about, some of them we don't. Well, what about it?'

It is instructive to observe that this particularly overt case of the human psychosis was in full agreement with Dr. John Robinson that God was something you found deep down in human relationships. He could also be made to assert that any reality human beings did not know about was unimportant, in fact unreal, because human beings did not know about it.

To complete this cameo of the human psychosis it is only necessary to observe that a study of this person's human relationships would undoubtedly have revealed a continuous indulgence in concealed sadism.[1]

\*

[1] I use the word 'sadism' for convenience, because there is no other (unless perhaps *Schadenfreude*) to express a psychological tendency to derive pleasure or gratification from damage done to other people, or suffering experienced

54

I must make it plain that the last thing which I mean to suggest is that the adult human personality can have any emotions about reality, or change itself in any significant way by thinking about it. No significant change is possible so long as the delusionary belief in the meaningfulness and altruistic nature of human activities remains intact.

Although it is to be presumed that the focus of emotional disturbance was once reality itself, this is no longer the case. As with other and lesser psychoses, the anxiety is too profound for its true locus even to be admitted; and the resistances must all be sought in a seemingly unrelated area.

The fundamental resistance has now become the resistance to the constellation of related ideas: (1) Human society is meaningless. (2) Human society is fundamentally sadistic. (3) My interest in other people is fundamentally sadistic.

*

Thus, as in the case already referred to, psychotics of this type will readily, in fact eagerly, admit that they are completely indifferent to reality. 'The reason for existence doesn't mean a thing to me . . .' – with a happy smile.

If, however, it is suggested that their true attitude to reality may be hatred rather than indifference, slightly more evidence of emotional involvement will appear. If the psychotic is reminded of those areas of reality most likely to arouse feelings of impotence, such as pain, disease, ageing, death, and so on, the suggestion that it would be possible for anyone to mind very much about any of these things will be rejected with slighting comments about the person who has made the suggestion. Emotionally loaded terms appear – 'moaning', 'whining', 'belly-aching', and so on. If this line of approach is continued, the psychotic may be made to show very definite signs of a hostile attitude to the observer, and remarks may be made which are revealing for the understanding of the structure of the psychosis, such as: 'Well, you're no worse off than anybody else'

by them. I do not, however, mean to imply that I suppose the pleasure or gratification involved is sexual in origin.

(in a vindictive tone of voice), or 'We're all in the same boat, so you can like it or lump it, can't you?' The form of these sentences, of course, implies that the observer has suggested that *he himself* minds very much about reality; but the sentences occur in this form even if the observer's remarks have been of the highest degree of impersonality.

*

The psychotic has no resistance to being told that he is obsessionally interested in other people, but he has maximal resistance to accepting that this interest arises from his hatred of them. If he accepted this he would, of course, have to say: 'Well, I want to hate people. I am not interested in the universe but I just want to hate people.' This would rob him of the fictitious social approval which is used to make his interest in other people (rationalised as 'altruism', 'fellow-feeling' and the like) safe from attack.

*

Now it is clear that before any change in human psychology, either individual or collective, could take place, it would be necessary for the belief in the meaningfulness of human society to be abandoned. (The resistance to its abandonment is of course immense.) It is true that this is only one of the attitudes which is invalidated by the perception of total uncertainty: but psychologically it is the lynch-pin of the whole affair. If you *never* believe that human society, or collective opinion, can confer any meaningfulness upon your actions or attitudes, you can never develop the human psychosis in a permanent form.

*

*An Example of Transposition*
There is a book called *Der Streit um den Sergeanten Grischa*.[1] This book is supposed to arouse deeply humanitarian feelings.
The hero, a prisoner of war, is trying to escape home to his

[1] Arnold Zweig, 1927; translated, under the title *The Case of Sergeant Grischa*, by Eric Sutton, Hutchinson International Authors, 1947.

wife and child (sacrosanct purpose-surrogates). He adopts a false identity, and in that identity is convicted of espionage. Although it is perfectly clear that he is not the man who committed espionage, the authorities insist on his execution.

We are given the impression of confronting a profound problem. Our indignation is aroused. We are made to feel that all will be well as soon as the human race only executes people who *have* committed espionage.

But the universe is condemning people to death all the time, and gives no reasons at all.

# CHAPTER 7

# Sadism

In the last chapter I outlined the form of the psychotic's resistance to the suggestion that his indifference to reality is not, perhaps, to be taken at face value.

It is more difficult to give an exhaustive classification of the psychotic's reactions to the suggestion that human psychology is in a state of which the primary motive is sadism. This is because the whole of psychotic society, one might almost say, is devoted to creating a climate in which it is impossible for the suggestion to be made or taken seriously. And, of course, there is a taboo on analytical thought in or near this area as I have mentioned before.

But I will describe one or two of the more characteristic reactions which prevent discussion from getting too near the point.

*

One is, at the first sign of a suggestion that the meaningfulness of human society is questionable, to say: 'Oh, I suppose you are suggesting we should all kill our grandmothers', or 'You don't have anything against murder, then.' This is often said in a noticeably aggressive tone, and the implication is plain: 'If it isn't enough for you that I *pretend* I don't hate people — if you don't leave my rationalisations intact — I'll show you.' The speed with which the psychotic leaps from 'there might be other criteria for action than social convention' to 'what everyone would really want to do in the absence of social convention is to kill people' is informative. A number of books have been written which have little interest on other grounds but which plainly play on precisely this aspect of the human psychosis.

They describe situations in which, for some reason, the constraints of civilisation are removed, and murder rapidly becomes commonplace. (I do not mean to suggest that these books are more uninteresting than other psychotic literature of a corresponding intellectual level. There is no reason why any of the cultural productions of a psychotic society should interest non-psychotics.)

As a further sidelight on this particular form of resistance, it may be mentioned that in discussing Nietzsche with psychotics one finds that they show an intense awareness of those portions of his writing in which he sanctions (or may be taken to sanction) cruelty to other humans.

It may well be, of course, that Nietzsche was not free of this reaction himself; he said 'I will see through human society', but did not distinguish between 'I am free to murder if I choose', and 'Murder is a thing that should be chosen'. This is only one among many distinctions which he failed to make explicit; though in every case of such a distinction it is clear that on some occasions he is meaning the one thing, and on other occasions the other. Nevertheless Nietzsche warrants attention as one of the infinitesimal number of people who have made a noticeable, even if only partially successful, attempt to liberate themselves from the human psychosis.

*

Another form of defence is for the psychotic to maintain that there is 'some good' in the world.

This is, in essence, an impenetrable defence, since no psychotic is willing to discuss 'goodness' on any terms other than those accepted by the generality of psychotics. It must be admitted as an undeniable proposition that the generality of people are no more miserable, bored, stultified, purposeless and vindictive than the generality of people.

However, by a certain effort of analysis, it is sometimes possible to establish that the generality of people are more miserable, bored, etc. than the ideal which the generality of people profess to hold. At this point the psychotic finds it important to assert that he has known someone – say a violinist in New York – who 'is very intense about his music'. Or perhaps it is an old lady who 'lives on frightfully little money, and is always giving things away'.

This demonstrates that the crucial issue, psychologically, is whether or not the situation is *totally* valueless. The psychotic can feel his position to be perfectly justified if, however indefensible the situation in general, there is or has been some person somewhere who, in at least some respect, lives up to the ideal (which the generality of people profess to hold).

*

In the paper today I observe that a man has committed suicide, first murdering his family. His social compensations having broken down what more natural than that he should at last feel free to express his hostility in the most direct way?

One might have felt free to do other things; but I have observed before that humans seem to identify 'freedom' with 'freedom to murder'.

Cf. Gide's 'actions gratuites' – a blow in the face in *Le Prométhée Mal Enchaîné*, a pointless murder in *Les Caves du Vatican*.

# CHAPTER 8

# Pleasure

There was a time when I had been living for a long time under continuous stress, as a result of the arrangements made by the human race for what was called my education, and I began to experience a craving for 'holidays'. I knew even at the time that if the stress were removed from my life I should want nothing less than a holiday, but I found myself dwelling upon an analgesic state in which one's mind would be so vacant, not only of conflict but of purpose also, that one would be able to pay attention to the goodness of things in relation to the class of things to which they happened to belong. (This, I believe, is the mental activity referred to as 'having pleasures'.) So, I would be able to think, 'I am having a walk and it is a nice walk as walks go', and 'that tree is a good sort of tree of the sort it is' and 'the grass is green and that is nice as green grass goes'.

However, I knew, as I have said, that this was not really possible for me and that the activity in question had no reality except in imagination. There is nothing in the process of 'having a pleasure' except the *imagination* of having a pleasure. Of course someone may *imagine* the process of taking pleasure in a nice cup of tea contemporaneously with drinking tea; but the apparent gratification arises from the *imagining* that accompanies the process; it is not inherent in the process itself. If ever you stop the imagining (which I suppose in most people must go on habitually) and look at what you are experiencing, asking what is *really* in it – you will see either the barrenness of human life or the astonishing fact of existence, depending on the efficiency of your psychological defences.

*

It is necessary, of course, to make a distinction between 'pleasures' and 'compensations'. No real gratification can be derived from 'pleasures', but there seems to be little doubt that people derive some kind of continuous gratification from 'compensations'. These are based upon the transference of aggression against one's limitations to 'other people', which gives rise to the ability to be gratified by the fact that they are limited.

*

It is quite possible that this introspective observation of mine sheds light on the significance of the concept of 'pleasure' as it commonly occurs in human psychology.

The differences arise from the fact that in the case of most people all conflicts which directly derive from their desire for the infinite are deeply buried in the subconscious; all that remains accessible to consciousness is the craving for relief. Needless to say, most people are not able to distinguish between what they imagine would be agreeable, and what they imagine is taking place in their lives. It is an easy step psychologically from imagining a certain process to identifying this imaginary process with others which are actually going on. There has been plenty of time for this psychological development to reach the completeness which is seen in the adult human, since it is clear that most people begin very early in life to give up their interest in the infinite.

*

Not only the concept of 'pleasure' derives its emotional significance from a relief-seeking process of this kind. The emotional tone associated with, say, the imaginary concept of 'human relationship' is derived in exactly the same way from the presence of continuous subconscious hostility. This explains the conjunction of sentimentality and sadism. (In its crudest forms, the existence of this conjunction has been remarked upon even by psychotic students of psychology.)

It will be observed that people who write treatises on the brotherhood of man and peace on earth are advocating the abolition of sadism by the cultivation of emotions which only sadists find interesting. As a man in continuous pain will ascribe a positive value to painlessness, though if he possessed it it would not preserve him from boredom or despair; so a person in a state of continuous hatred may well come to ascribe a positive value to an absence of hatred; and a world where communication is impossible may talk a great deal about 'exchanging ideas' and 'dialogue'.

It follows, by not too devious a train of thought, that in actual fact the human race will have wars so long as it glorifies altruism.

# CHAPTER 9

# Ageing

Since everyone elects to adopt such an anthropocentric position, it follows that the most potent reminder of their finiteness must be provided by the process of ageing. (If people did not adopt such an anthropocentric position they might experience their finiteness in the form of claustrophobia at being unable to visualise the fourth dimension, or to conceive of infinity.)

From about the age of twenty-five, or from whatever age an irreversible deterioration is first noticeable in their physical organism, the psychological adjustment of the sane human must undergo a profound change. In fact, some such age is recognised to be that of the onset of 'maturity' or 'responsibility', and society is so arranged that people are subject to the restrictive control of persons who have passed the age of twenty-five until they themselves reach, or nearly reach, this age. It is then confidently assumed that physiological processes will take over the restrictive function.

There is every sign that the human race has a great resistance to admitting what is really going on. No hint is given to children or adolescents that from the age of twenty-five onwards they may expect to conduct their lives under the gloom of an irreversible process of decay. No one publicises the early age (usually not later than the early twenties) at which most people begin to find their outlook blighted by the first signs of balding, wrinkles, rheumatics, and so on. Every attempt is made to talk children out of any sense of urgency they may possess by presenting 'adulthood' as a great expanse of future time which will be just as good as the present for doing things in.

It is of course quite unthinkable to a non-psychotic mind that the reaction to the awareness of such irreversible processes can be the characteristic syndrome of 'adulthood'. This syndrome does not appear to find it necessary to react to these reminders of its finite condition by wasting less time, by stripping its life of purposeless activities. On the contrary, the concept of pleasure seems to become more meaningful than ever before and the tendency to waste time is even more universal.

It is clear, since psychology must react in some way to the pall of gloom which begins to come upon it at the age of about twenty-five, that if its reaction does not take the form of urgency and purposefulness, it must take that of viciousness to other humans, and particularly of course to those who do not live in the obsessional awareness of ageing (in referring to the 'obsessional awareness', I realise that the awareness is repressed as totally as possible; but it is impossible to suppose that it is not present, and present as a determining factor of most adult motivation).

Indeed, the strength of the resistance is shown by the fact that no psychoanalyst to my knowledge has referred, say, to the jealousy of parents who are just beginning to pass the prime of life for their as yet untarnished offspring. Only sexual forms of jealousy are ever discussed. If the jealousy of a mother for her grown-up daughter, or father for son, is presented as a literary or psychoanalytic theme, it is presented purely in terms of sexual competition. It is never suggested that the older person would automatically feel jealousy for any consciousness into which no pre-occupation with irreversible deterioration has yet entered.

The conclusion seems unavoidable that purely physical jealousy must govern the attitudes of the human race, both as individuals and collectively, towards the young.

This will only be overt in the case of those children who show serious signs of living intensely or purposefully. It is most important that they should waste their time until they reach an age when purely physiological considerations will result in a sense of impotence and frustration. It is assumed that they will, in such circumstances, abandon their drive to transcend.

This, of course, is an almost universally correct assumption.

People might react to ageing with urgency, but it would have to be an extreme urgency. By the time they reach the operative age, society will have conditioned into them many attitudes which will preclude any possibility of *that*.

# CHAPTER 10

# Fiction

In view of the facts of the situation, how do people live? The contents of their minds are unimaginable. But after a time one arrives at the conclusion that, whatever these contents may be, they certainly include a belief in their own survival of death. The fact that everyone *emotionally* believes this is entirely independent of any views on the matter which they may openly profess. It is clear that everyone is behaving *as though* they are going to live for ever. This is the only way in which their lack of any sense of urgency can be made comprehensible. And, furthermore, they do not believe that ageing is an irreversible process. Emotionally they regard it as a temporary episode.

The fact that they are able to believe such things is part of what I mean by their assumption that their life is fictional. I once knew someone who said that when she read novels, for example, her emotional reaction to them was that to read of other people's experience of life was providing her with additional degrees of freedom. It was as if she could enter the life of any of them, including herself, at any point she chose. This reveals that her own life had to her the status of fiction; she had never taken it seriously as fact. Now this I believe must be universally true. Children fulfil much the same function as novels in providing people with a fictional extension of their own existence.

There is another sense in which everyone lives as though their lives were fictional. They live as though they were quite sure their actions had no consequences, and could not affect anything that mattered outside the range of ideas which they choose to present to themselves as being 'what the story is about'. It is as if they were quite sure they were characters in a book, and had no need to think of what might lie beyond its covers. A person might read the book, but none of the characters need do anything else but go on thinking of their story-book affairs.

Now to find it adequate to *imagine* something, or to pretend that it is so, without feeling concern as to whether it is true or not, is related to unawareness of the total uncertainty. It is impossible to have a feeling for reality as something that exists independently of what one imagines about it, without becoming aware of the total uncertainty, and *vice versa*.

No one who was aware of the total uncertainty would be able to believe in survival, nor would he be able to content himself by imagining throughout his life that it was so.

Of course the intellectual forms in which the underlying emotional belief expresses itself may be very complex. Now that religion is no longer fashionable, there is a complicated way of proving to yourself that you do not need to worry about dying, as once you are dead you will not know that you are. This obviously has exactly the same reassuring properties as were once possessed by pictures of angels with harps. Clearly what it is doing is to establish an emotional correspondence between the propositions: 'I will never know that I have died' – 'If I pretend I am immortal nothing will ever be able to disturb the pretence' – 'So long as I am alive I shall always be able to pretend that I am immortal' – 'I am immortal.'

Recently I knew of someone who was given fourteen weeks to live. It is perfectly clear that his reaction to this situation depended entirely on maintaining the fiction that he was never going to die. This was almost explicit in the way in which he set about seeking the most fashionable cancer cures wherever they might be found, instead of deciding that he would need the whole of the fourteen weeks to think about dying without materialistic interruptions.

The fictional attitude was also implicit in the way in which, up to the very last, he went on 'taking an interest' in letters from members of his family about their affairs, and in having the lives of statesmen read to him. What was the use to him of news about the antics of his infant nephew, or of sidelights on the

68

political weakness of Lord So-and-So? Except, of course, to maintain the fiction that in some sense he was not uniquely bound up in the fate of his own consciousness.

After a certain length of time – a little less than fourteen weeks – he died. The human race, which sets no great store by realism, expressed its admiration of his attitude. 'His courage has been an example to us all,' they said; and went away to the Bahamas to recover.

CHAPTER 11

# Friendship

I do not know if you are acquainted with the *Reader's Digest*. I used to read it at one time because it is a convenient thing to obtain in a number of languages. Also, perhaps, since there are no such things as magazines designed for people like me, it is as well to read something that is so unequivocally disagreeable that it may be read as a parody of itself.

It seems to me a remarkable guide to the contents of the normal mind. There can be little doubt that every item is selected for the universality of its appeal. (It boasts a readership of five million people.) Consider a few of the items I noticed. (I shall quote from the French edition – my translation.)

First an article about a letter from a dear old friend. It is all, of course, written in a cosily humorous tone. But the question is whether such reactions would even appear amusing to people who did not have them. The writer of the article receives a letter from the aforesaid dear old friend, and finds it difficult to formulate a reply – which is not surprising, since he has no genuine motive for replying at all. His social conventions evidently forbid his writing to his dear old friend to say: 'I am getting awfully conflicted about writing to you because I am not really motivated to do so.' Instead, he has to go on trying. Soon he starts to have thoughts about his dear old friend which are not only hostile but hostile in the established patterns of sane psychology.

> I ended up taking a dislike to Walter. Who did he think he was to inflict such a torture on me? What right did he have to complicate my existence with his smart and superficial letter? You could soon see that Walter Brenner did not have my worries. In fact, he had never had them. No doubt he was still living in the same tree-lined avenue in the same big

white house which had seen him born. No mortgages for him, no running to catch trains. He must think that I was possessed of an infinite amount of leisure to chatter with him interminably by letter. The difficulty into which he had put me had already lasted for weeks. Yes, he had spoilt whole weeks for me by his irresponsiblity. Walter Brenner had certainly always had a gift for making life impossible for you.[1]

Observe here the jealousy, the theme of 'what right has he to interfere with my individuality?', the theme of 'why should he have more advantages than me?', and the assumption that the most advantageous situation in life would be one of complete 'leisure' and vacuity.

Eventually, the problem is solved when the author's wife composes a letter for him to his friend Walter. The author cleverly adds to this letter just those words which place his friend under an obligation to write again and so exposes him to the same conflicts which the author has himself just experienced.

> I felt as if an enormous weight had just been lifted from my shoulders. In a burst of tenderness and gratitude, I kissed my marvellous wife and, for the first time in long weeks, I was again at peace with the world . . .
>
> I liked to think that I was now able to show myself equal to the situation. I took my pen and added at a stroke: '. . . when I hear from you again'.
>
> After that, I plunged into my arm-chair with a smile on my lips. A splendid friend, Walter! His turn to suffer now![2]

Another article, about life in the wilds of Alaska, contains a gloating description of some rather crude surgery carried out on an Eskimo who had been mauled by a bear. I do not believe that any part of the content of the *Reader's Digest* is accidental. It is precisely geared to what people want to read. So consider what motivation could make anyone want to read the following:

> At the bottom of the boat lay the other traveller, more dead than alive, his clothes and body all torn and lacerated.
>
> 'He went into the forest in pursuit of a wounded bear,' said the boy.

[1] Charlton Ogburn, 'Torture par Correspondance', *Sélection du Reader's Digest*, December, 1966, p. 210.
[2] Ibid., p. 212.

I might have guessed as much. It is easy to recognise a man who has been maltreated by a bear . . .

He screamed and lost consciousness, which was just as well for him, since I had not even begun to sew up his face.

I was going to use caribou nerve, but Cecelia said that it would rot in the skin and come undone. She suggested I should use some hair taken from the Eskimo's head. So I tore a fist-full of hair from him . . . Then I looked hard at the man's head, wondering how best to begin sewing him up. Till then, the youth had followed my every movement, helping me as best he could. But, when I brought together two pieces of the wounded man's mouth and plunged the needle into the flesh, he ran towards the bushes and I heard him being sick.[1]

But the *coup de grâce* is yet to come. The man who was sewn up is called Henry, and he recovers. Some time later the author of this story meets a friend of Henry's.

'How is your friend Henry?' I soon asked him.

Immediately there was silence in the igloo and the young man shook his head sadly.

'At the beginning of winter,' he said, 'Henry took a team of dogs onto the river. The ice was still very fragile, but no one could make him listen to reason. He fell straight in, not far from here, with his dogs, his sledge and everything. We found nothing but the hole in the ice.'

This news made me angry. I might as well not have taken all that trouble to save the fellow.[2]

Now I repeat that I am sure that everything in the *Reader's Digest* is there because it is maximally easy for the maximum number of people to identify with it. We must therefore believe that this is a reaction with which many people could identify themselves. I.e. on hearing of someone's death, you think: 'He couldn't even take the trouble to keep alive after I went out of my way to do something for him!' Now other reactions to the situation would be possible. For example, one might think: 'How awful that after one terrible experience he should meet his death in such a claustrophobic way.' But, of course, this is perilously near to the thought: 'Finiteness is altogether intoler-

[1] James Huntingdon, 'Aux Frontières de l'Inconnu', *Sélection du Reader's Digest*, December 1966, pp. 249–50.

[2] Ibid., p. 254.

72

able and nothing one can do is sufficient to control the situation.' In fact, this example provides an almost explicit instance of the displacement of hostility from the objective situation on to some other person. Instead of thinking: 'Even my efforts to save his life could not prevent him from death on another occasion. I am impotent,' the author thinks: 'He did not value my efforts highly enough to take the trouble to remain alive.'

It may be observed, both in this story and in the article about the letter from Walter, how extremely aware normal people are of the trouble to which they go for one another and how excessive and unjustifiable they feel it to be that the slightest demand to vary the purposelessness of their lives should be made on them by any other person.

# CHAPTER 12

# Laughter

A young graduate who had read English at Oxford and with whom I was corresponding once referred to *jokes* about ageing. Certainly they are common.

The first thing one notices about them is that they all depend on the implicit or explicit introduction of 'other people' into the situation. In some way or another, they all say, 'I am living out a life-cycle as other people have done before, or as my contemporaries are also doing now.' I do not think you could make a joke out of being the first or only person to find himself enmeshed in the conditions of mortality.

Two questions arise: what makes this reference to the widespread occurrence of mortality *funny*, and how is one to account for its sedative effect? (Plainly, the effect of the joke is one of reconciliation to the situation, rather than a spur to action.)

Freud would no doubt claim that the funniness arose from the reference to an underlying anxiety. The behaviourists would no doubt say that a thing was funny if accompanied by the action of laughing. I don't feel particularly enlightened by either suggestion. There is only one nonsane joke: it is about attempting the impossible. It is extremely hilarious, but I do not think that it resembles any form of sane funniness. There is one other existential form of laughter: this is the laughter of relief. Again, I cannot feel that it sheds light on sane humour.

Quite possibly there are at least two kinds of funniness; perhaps they include both the humour of anxiety and the humour of relief. I do not find this possibility disturbing because, unlike the behaviourists, I find no difficulty in supposing that a given set of motor actions may correspond to a number of different psychological events.

Incidentally, it is just possible that a person in a state of existential awareness might find it funny to be the only person to die. This would be a variant of the joke about attempting the impossible. But he would not bother to draw anyone's attention to it.

However, I will hazard a guess why sane people make jokes about growing old. What the joke means is 'I am as degraded as everybody else, but at least everybody else is as degraded as I am.' This is *funny* in the same way that other references to one's concealed hatred of other people are funny, and it explains why the joke functions as a sedative. ('At least I can see everyone else rotting at the same time I do; at least I can hear them screaming while I'm being tortured myself . . .')

Come to think of it, does not all sane humour depend on references to one's concealed hatred of other people? My studies of the *Reader's Digest* certainly suggest this. 'Human relationships' seem to consist of continual reminders that your 'friend' sees you as identified with your most degrading limitations. (But loves you just the same, of course. That is, he *wants* you to be like that.)

There is an interesting piece of linguistic usage in this area. 'To value someone as an individual' is supposed to mean 'to wish him to be just as he is; to want him to be just that unique person with all his weaknesses and contradictions.' If I ever say that what I would mean by valuing an individual would be to value him as an aspiring entity, and not to identify him with any contingent limitation – people turn upon me with an indignantly blazing eye, and say, 'You mean you want to *use* people.'

Do not ask me to explain the logical relevance of this remark; I report its occurrence in this context as a fact of psychology.

# CHAPTER 13

# Mental Health

I see that even sane people no longer claim that the defining characteristic of their state is realisticness or rationality. I observe that sanity has been defined as 'a tendency to avoid extreme views'. And a booklet on mental health says that the mentally ill person 'just doesn't react to things the way a normal person would.'[1]

I don't know that I quite like the honesty that is coming over the human race in this region. Didn't they use to define sanity as 'a tendency to avoid unrealistic views' or 'not to react to things in an irrational and illogical fashion'?

It is clear that on the present definition I could not defend my sanity for one moment, and I don't really see why the human race doesn't take me away at once and give me ECT daily for the rest of my life. I don't see it has any ethics of a kind to prevent it.

What is interesting about this definition is that it actually classes philosophically realistic people as *insane* even more inescapably than it classes, say, paranoids as *insane*. The situation in which we find ourselves is an extreme one. Realistic views will, of necessity, be extreme. A paranoid is not so extreme as a realist; in fact, his views may not be extreme at all. I do not see anything too startling in the belief that people are trying to poison one. They might be. It would not affect our views on the laws of nature at all if it turned out that they were.

Of course, if one *really* wanted to make a distinction between a sane and an insane opinion, one would have to take the motivation into account. If a person, out of no motive but a desire to arrive at the most probable interpretation of the facts,

[1] Richard Christner, 'A *positive* approach to Mental Health', National Association for Mental Health, 1965.

76

concluded that people were trying to poison him, I should not regard his realism as discredited, although I should not feel myself obliged to accept his conclusion if a different assessment of the facts appeared to me more probable. But if it was clear that he was motivated to believe that people were trying to poison him because he wanted to remain in a certain kind of emotional position relative to other people, then I should not consider his conclusion a realistic one – even if they were trying to poison him.

However, a distinction of this kind could not safely be made by sane people, on the stones-and-glass-houses principle. Their own beliefs – about the psychology of other people and about everything else – are dictated by their desire to remain in certain emotional positions, facts regardless.

As I say, they used to claim that their position was dictated by realism and rationality. This was fairly safe because few people were likely to point out that it wasn't. But, it is true, their position is even more unassailable if it is openly based on the statistical norm.

When they come to take me away there will be nothing I can say. 'I am perfectly rational about coordinate geometry,' I will say. 'Let me prove a few theorems for you. I am particularly clear-headed about the fourth dimension. I can discourse on the concepts of theoretical physics with perfect clarity even if not with social acclaim. I can make any well-known physicist contradict himself within five minutes. Theologians within two minutes. I can play chess and write out the Hebrew alphabet. I can tell you the word for 'nevertheless' in Swedish, and twenty words for 'significance' in German . . .'

But it will all be beside the point. 'Enough of that,' they will say grimly. *'You just don't react to things the way a normal person does.'*

*

I have just seen another definition of insanity: a condition of retreat from *society*. Not from reality, you observe. What does human society think it is – Emerson's Brahma, or something?

77

Personally I give mad elephants as wide a berth as possible.

Incidentally, this definition illustrates the human prescription for living: collective presumption and individual humility. (Humility meaning: willingness to be pushed around by society.) If an *individual* said: 'Anyone who doesn't want to know me is mad' – this would be regarded as megalomania and no one would stop to examine the grounds on which he said it. If *society* says: 'If you don't want anything to do with me you're mad' – the grounds for the statement aren't examined either, but no one gives society a bad mark. (And, indeed, how unthinkable that an *individual* should venture to judge the utterances of *society*.)

# CHAPTER 14

# Solipsism

Having once presented some arguments in favour of the contention that life might (for all one knew to the contrary) be illusory, I was asked 'whether I believed in solipsism'. This, of course, was said with a slight sneer, as though anyone who entertained such a *belief* was known to be risible. (It may be mentioned that I was in what might pass for philosophically sophisticated company.)

I said I accepted the irrefutability of solipsism. This produced expressions of incredulity and a total lack of response, as if I had said something incredible or meaningless.

*

Now it is known that very curious considerations suffice to support people in *believing* that life is not hallucinatory. Professor Broad, and others, have found it difficult to disbelieve in the existence of external objects when they thought about the resistance which they experienced on pushing and pulling them.[1] (And yet, of course, people experience this kind of resistance sometimes when they pull and push things in lucid dreams – if you need such evidence that hallucinatory pushing and pulling is a logical possibility.)[2]

But there seems little doubt what it is that has the greatest potency in eliminating from consideration any doubts about the

[1] Cf. C. D. Broad, *Religion, Philosophy and Psychical Research,* Routledge and Kegan Paul, 1953, p. 34; discussed in my book, *The Human Evasion,* Institute of Psychophysical Research, 1969, pp. 81–2.

[2] A lucid dream is a dream in which the subject is aware that he is dreaming; cf. my book *Lucid Dreams*, Institute of Psychophysical Research, 1968.

status of one's life. It is *other people*. It may be difficult to doubt the real existence of physical objects that one can pull and push. How much more difficult to doubt the real existence of *people* who seem able to recognise one's own existence, confer significance upon one by their agreement — and so forth.

And yet clearly the focal point of the human evasion is not the belief that other people exist, but the belief that other people exist *and* are an unquestionable repository of value.

The belief is usually stated in the form: people are rational and compassionate and in general are to be taken at face value, and no one can doubt the value of a nice compassionate rational human being, because all human beings have always agreed in believing that the value of this cannot be doubted.

However, the psychological force of the argument is probably, more centrally: people can confer significance upon me, and I ought to believe that they can, because everyone has always agreed in believing that human beings were the most valuable things to human beings. I.e. people talk as if they are recognising the valuableness of other people, but what they really mean is that they want other people to confer significance on them.

# CHAPTER 15

# The Hypothetical

The human race has no tolerance of the hypothetical. It likes to turn hypotheses into opinions. It does not matter at all if someone believes that you hold an opinion about the situation which is diametrically opposed to their own, but it seems that the concept of a permanent, irrefutable, and yet uncertain hypothesis occasions them discomfort.

This is a curious and intriguing feature of human psychology, which I believe has hitherto escaped comment.

To illustrate what I mean, suppose that you are discussing solipsism with somebody. You point out that it is an irrefutable possibility that no one other than yourself has a consciousness. He will immediately start discussing this as if you had asserted your personal belief that no one other than yourself has a consciousness. (He, almost certainly, will have a quite definite personal belief that everyone who seems to have a consciousness actually has one.)

Similarly, if you point out the vast quantity of possibilities which are constantly left out of account by the human race in running its affairs on a basis of pseudo-omniscience, he will not be in the least interested in all the irrefutably possible possibilities which you may bring to light, but only in trying to guess at some system of dogmatic belief, different from his own, which he would like to believe you believe in.

It might be supposed that this lack of interest in the concept of the hypothetical might stem from lack of adequate mental resources. There is, presumably, a level of intelligence below which the notion of a permanent but unproven possibility is difficult to grasp. However, this desire to discuss only *beliefs* is found in people of the highest supposed intelligence, so it must be supposed that the preference is emotional. There is an almost audible sigh of relief, an almost visible sinking back onto restful accustomed cushions, when your interlocutor can persuade you to express a personal preference for one side of the possible alternatives. Even if, be it noted, this is only a tentative preference it removes the matter from the realm of fact. It is no longer necessary to discuss the facts, as such, at all. We can discuss it all in terms of 'I think so and so . . .' 'Well, myself, I think so and so . . .' 'I believe in reincarnation, actually, and I think domestic animals go to heaven, but not wild ones.' 'Do you really? Well, myself, I don't think *all* domestic animals go to heaven, but I think there is a special part of heaven set aside for the wild animals . . .' and so on.

A final refinement of this state of affairs should be noted. People not only want you to *believe* things (and not just entertain hypotheses, or be aware of possibilities), but they want you to *disbelieve* their own beliefs. If you do not, for example, absolutely believe in reincarnation, and they do, they do not want you to say that you do not reject the possibility of reincarnation. They want you to be *hostile* to reincarnation, and keep putting words into your mouth until they have convinced themselves that you are.

# CHAPTER 16

# The Fear of Failure (I)

I am not too sure what the human race means by 'balanced'. I have some idea what *I* might mean by unbalanced, having had employees at various times who were liable without warning to take off into the wide blue yonder, or to be found mildly off their rockers muttering feverishly to themselves in their bed-sitters. But in the sense in which I could never possibly contrive to be 'balanced' enough to satisfy anybody, I didn't feel I understood it. (Of course, it is a very useful and practical idea not to define your pejorative terms too distinctly. Then you can attack who you like.)

But I see that until I was ten I was more like socially acceptable people I knew at college, and that the characteristic elements of my psychology that always aroused opposition were not yet present. So maybe I might have passed as balanced, but it was totally fallacious to think I could be steered through the whole of my education on those terms.

Up to the age of ten I had no sufficiently clear idea of how I wanted to be living to be dissatisfied with what was set before me. I did what was set before me because it was set before me, and not because of any principle of selection of my own. I did not reflect on the fact that I wasn't learning much at school because I knew it all already. I did whatever other children did, up to a point, to pass the time, so I seemed as nearly normal as I ever would.

The things I tried to do on my own were such as, with some encouragement, might have led to a sort of intellectual intensity which would immediately have made a lower intensity of living unsatisfactory, but I did not realise this, nor recognise a deliberate policy in people's deflecting me from such things. (I acquired, for example, a French novel and the first part of an elementary course in French and attempted to decipher the novel. But the part of the French course was an extremely incomplete guide to the grammar and vocabulary of the language as a whole, and nobody gave me a dictionary.)

If asked what I wanted to do in life, I would have said I wanted to be a scientist, and do research, but I wouldn't have been very clear whether the sort of science I would like best was more likely to be found under the heading of physics or chemistry, and (which now seems quite odd) even if people had tried to convince me that if I didn't get the grammar school scholarship I would never be allowed to do research, I do not think it would have seemed to me a matter of life and death. In fact, I didn't regard the grammar school scholarship as a necessary stage on the way to doing research, and anyway I could imagine doing other things in life.

Nor had it dawned upon me that it was a very uninteresting question whether someone with my ability, at the advanced age of ten, could pass a thing like a scholarship, and that only getting a hundred per cent in everything would really be any expression of what I was. And, in this felicitous unawareness, I got a hundred per cent in everything.

But it may be observed that the unawareness which preserved me from conflict in this case depended on a combination of inexperience and living in an un-intense (not to say bored) way. There was no possibility that I could take a degree, ten years later, on the same terms.

But it seems to me that I knew people who did, more or less. They went on doing what society set before them without ever acquiring inconveniently demanding internal criteria of their own, and though social success seemed to them quite desirable, and being in the academic world quite agreeable, the possibility of being outside of it didn't seem to them intolerable, either. Which is, of course, a very fortunate psychological position to be in.

*

Once when I was thirteen I had been having one of my philosophical discussions with a certain nun who taught in a convent school that I was attending at the time; it had no doubt centred around the question of whether you could find intellectual pursuits and research unnecessary if you ascribed the right sort of primacy to human relationships. Finally, she turned and said to me, 'But intelligence isn't everything. There are other qualities that count. No three-year-old could possibly do Upper Third work.'

'Why should she want to think that is impossible?' I wondered. 'Maybe there are limiting factors on the degree of precocity that is possible, but I don't know them. The human race is evolving; I suppose it is more intelligent on the whole than when it lived in caves . . .'

So I didn't answer, and doubtfully considered the question.

'Even if it were intelligent enough it wouldn't have the maturity,' she said.

I wasn't very sure what the factor of maturity would be supposed to consist of, so I considered that also.

'Well, do you agree or don't you?' she said sharply.

'Oh, yes,' I said untruthfully.

'You're not marvellous, you know,' she said. 'You're quite good, but you're not an Einstein.'

I perceived that I didn't like that, although I had never thought of being an Einstein. I had only thought of myself as doing research and being the dullest and most industrious sort of researcher, and if I had identified at all with any degree of famousness, I suppose I might have thought I might conceivably one day creep into the textbooks as the sort of person who rates one mention for devising a different shape of airhole for a Bunsen burner. Nevertheless, it is true that I wanted to do theoretical physics, and one didn't like to think that everything one could ever think about physics would always be limited to a degree of insignificance specifiable in advance. One wanted to work very hard, basically, so as to feel alive, but there was always the hope of surprising oneself. And I saw that if you thought of yourself as a certain sort of person who could only do unsurprising things it could all feel not worthwhile.

*

As people have sometimes observed in other contexts, to do anything well it is desirable (and may be essential) to be able to envisage the possibility of failure.

In non-intellectual contexts this is accepted. It is understood that the very young Wimbledon aspirant is at a psychological advantage in a match with an established champion, who is expected to win and will appear ridiculous if she doesn't; whereas the new arrival will be exceeding expectations if she wins.

When I was beginning, after not taking the School Certificate, to be distressed by my disconnection from my work, I tried to express the disorientation and lack of confidence that this produced. But, I was told, if you worked steadily (which was described as a completely mechanical process) you would acquire a sense of mastery. I wouldn't have said that that was a feeling I had ever had when I was feeling good about things, more a sense of taking risks that it was right to be taking; but now of course I tried to have it. On this theory, the objective was an unwavering confidence which prevented you from ever envisaging the prospect of failure.

When failure cannot be envisaged it is difficult to be motivated at all, and this difficulty is greater in relation to some faculties than others.

It is very difficult to attempt ESP[1] or PK[2]. We may hazard a guess that if people tried and failed, they would be made too much aware of their finiteness. People are, as we know, in a condition of finiteness to which they are apparently not reacting and which they apparently do not mind.

*

When I took the grammar school scholarship I struck up an

---

[1] Extrasensory perception      [2] Psychokinesis

acquaintanceship with a little girl in a mustard dress, and in the break after the arithmetic paper she said she thought it had been very easy and she had done well. Afterwards I told my mother this, and she said, 'Oh, well, she hadn't. Those that really have never say things like that.'

So I assumed provisionally that she was right, and that people who had done well never thought they had, but as time passed the psychology involved came to have a much more direct significance to me.

Certainly in my first years at the convent I could never believe that I had done well in any exam. I knew that it was incumbent upon me to come top, again and again and again, but while I could sometimes believe that I might have managed to score some marks, in order to come top it was necessary to believe that everybody else without exception would score fewer, and as what I did was of the utmost simplicity and obviousness, and some of them were after all quite intelligent, this strained my imaginative capacity to the utmost.

I remember one particularly harrowing arithmetic paper on which I concentrated so totally that I could trace afterwards no recollection of having checked or confirmed what I was doing, or stopped to convince myself that I was not doing everything all wrong. I was agonised at the thought that I might have scored no marks at all, or maybe a few here or there for method, but could I be sure there was any sense in my method? Perhaps I had multiplied the division sums, and so forth. I was incredulous when I found I had a hundred per cent.

Maths, I soon decided, was far the worst for this sort of thing. Of course, the sort of concentration I went in for did not always produce this kind of quasi-amnesia. When I took the grammar school scholarship it left me, instead, with an almost complete memory of the exact figures that had been set in each sum, and the answers I had obtained, so that when I got home my parents were able to work through the sums and confirm that I had them right.

But I hadn't thought the grammar school scholarship mattered in any way, but at the convent, at least in the early years, I was aware of the hostility of the girls towards me, which was held at bay only by my coming incessantly top.

I am under the impression that maths is, and not only in my own experience, the subject most liable to produce these psychological effects. I knew several people who did extremely well in their maths degrees, but were nevertheless under the impression that they had failed or got Fourths.

So in order to be able to approach mathematics in the right way, it is necessary to be able to convince yourself that success or failure is not of great importance to you, whether the conviction is realistic or unrealistic, and with any degree of conscious or subconscious dishonesty, so long as it works. Actually all the people I am thinking of did have very obvious escape clauses in their outlooks, two being Christians and none very much interested in the academic world.

(Incidentally, what I have just said of mathematics is, I rather think, even more quintessentially and ineluctably true of doing ESP deliberately. A degree of semi-deliberate self-deception that may pass for mathematics won't do for ESP.)

Well, of course, when I arrived at college my psychological condition was, *vis à vis* the doing of mathematics, quite dreadful. But it was impossible to convince myself that the consequences of failure were unimportant, because they included being regarded as socially disqualified from doing research. On this point my psychological ingenuity foundered.

I have not, since leaving college, so conducted my life that nightmarishness has been a frequent sensation, but on the few occasions that I have felt anything like it I have thought how obvious it was that it blocked thought. Robert Louis Stevenson describes a state of panic in *Kidnapped*; as there not being any time to think, like a man running.[1]

Recently, out of curiosity, I looked at a set of exercises in a book of solid geometry which I had been mesmerised by in my first year at college. My state at that time was such that a problem terrified me if there were not an obvious and mechani-

[1] Cf. *Kidnapped*, Sphere Books, 1972, p. 61.

cal method for beginning to solve it. And there was one problem in particular for which there was no such obvious method, so that I had stared at it in horror for some time before deciding not to attempt it. So I thought I would try to do it now, and of course I saw the solution in about a minute, and it only took a line or so to write it down.

\*

Now of course you may think that anyone who can be reduced to a state of nightmare and horror by being frustrated in their education, and by the impending threat of expulsion for life from the academic world, to such an extent that the expression of their abilities is impaired, rightfully deserves that the said horrific fate shall befall them.

However, one might point out that in the case of the genuinely precocious the ages at which it is natural to do certain kinds of thing are actually different from the accepted norm, and a very considerable sense of dislocation can result from retardation.

Then again, if one is precocious in the way I was, one knows exactly what one wants in life at a very early age, and if this is separated by a very large number of years from the age at which it is socially acceptable to start doing it, a long period results in which one is very vulnerable to those who play upon one's fear that, ultimately, society might not regard one as good enough. People find it amusing to play upon this fear in the case of someone who is exceptionally highly adapted to certain pursuits, and finds it impossible to imagine living without them.

The risk is lessened if one is less precocious, or if one's precocity does not include a clear awareness of the horrific consequences of ultimate failure, or if one is not the sort of person who arouses people's desire to torment. (I.e. if one is less obviously exceptional.)

If one were required to perform a certain moderately tricky high dive, failure to perform which correctly enough would result in execution by firing squad, it might be desirable to get on with it, and not to spend a preliminary ten years having to listen to people describing to one all the ways in which one might do it wrong, and exactly what execution by firing squad might be like.

# CHAPTER 17

# The Fear of Failure (II)

After I had not taken the School Certificate everyone became very interested in assessing me. I became aware that everything I did was regarded as material on which assessments of my ability would be based, not as something which indicated how I might improve.

I wasn't allowed to do the things I wanted to do, such as more subjects; and I was made to do things I didn't want to do at all, such as sitting through English lessons with 'my own age group'. I couldn't be allowed to go to a French play with the Arts Sixth Form because I was in the Science Sixth Form and if I missed the merest fraction of a maths lesson it would be impossible to assess me properly in comparison with the other people doing maths.

But I was given vaguely to understand that if I were assessed with sufficient thoroughness I might, if the assessment were sufficiently favourable, one day be given a bit more of something I wanted; and given distinctly to understand that if I didn't find the prospect of being assessed entirely adequate as a motive for working to the limits of my capacity, I was a depraved coward and weakling (which was, in the case of somebody like me, very probable).

I found the situation oppressive and claustrophobic; it is difficult now to know how clearly I formulated to myself that that feeling arose from a disbelief that they would give me anything I found pleasant anyway. I was trying not to know it; I wanted to feel motivated to work; if I could work enough I would feel more alive.

But assessment only meant that they wanted to define in advance what one could, and especially couldn't, do in all the rest of one's life. Conscientious I might try to be, but I perceived my energies ebbing. Not trying wasn't an acceptable excuse, they had told one in advance. But the not trying was involuntary, even so. Apparently the operative part of one's mind wouldn't make the effort to do something of which the only outcome was to be the defining of limitations.

*

I first started to think about the psychology of ESP during my first year at college. It happened that there was a copy of Myers's *Human Personality*[1] in Somerville library. This was the first time I had realised that any serious work had been done in this sort of field, and so the first time I had considered it, however tentatively, as a possible subject of research.

I was still very uncertain how the apparent evidence was to be regarded, but I began to speculate about ESP. It seemed most plausible that it was a latent faculty prevented from conscious use by emotional resistances rather than a peculiarity of a few odd members of the human race.

But if people tried to do ESP and failed, it would prove that they couldn't. Everyone was brought up to regard it as something that couldn't be done, but so long as they didn't try, it didn't prove it. (I mean, of course, this is how it would probably appear on the level of motivation that was really operative. Trying and failing would actually only prove that, on a certain occasion and in a specific set of psychological circumstances, they had failed.)

They might think they were trying, of course, in experiments or if they had a strong enough reason, but perhaps this was analogous to the conscientious conscious trying that wasn't really any good for doing maths if the genuine motivation wasn't there. The part of the mind that really had to be motivated in order to do maths properly withheld itself; perhaps the part that did ESP did the same.

At this time I tried to do some card-guessing. I tried concen-

[1] F. W. H. Myers, *Human Personality,* Longmans, Green & Co., London, 1903.

trating in different ways, but I was no more capable of scoring above chance than anybody else I knew.

*

Let me tell you how to do ESP.

First you need to have an idea of a sort of psychological decision-making position. Imagine that you are the President of the United States deciding whether to do something that may deter the Russians from blowing the world up, or alternatively may provoke them to do it. The fate of the world inevitably depends upon what you decide. Nobody can tell you what to do. You cannot afford to make a mistake.

In such a situation you may find yourself referring to some sort of internal feeling of rightness.

I do not, of course, suggest that if you are trying to do ESP you should make any attempt to dramatise the importance of what you are doing; that would be very inhibitory. The point of the example just given is to try to define a psychological position, which actually needs to be understood as exactly as possible, and is only likely to be clearly defined in situations which are heavily loaded.

In addition to being in this decision-making position, you also need to be as detached as possible from conflict-producing implications. But detachment is understood in many misleading ways; actually, I don't mean anything by it that cannot be produced by a good deal of analytical thought. In summary, it can be produced by becoming aware of the fact that existence is existing, i.e. that the whole situation in which one finds oneself is intrinsically inconceivable.

This, by reference to past analysis, may have the effect of considerably reducing the force of the idea that ESP is improbable, or that it makes a great deal of difference to the extraordinariness of the situation whether ESP exists or not.

You then watch the contents of your mind. Reject anything obviously coloured with a motive or association and try again. Genuine impressions tend to be very uncoloured, neutral, almost not there. Remember William James's definition of a 'gap in consciousness' – what you are aware of when you are just on the verge of remembering a word, and know everything about what it feels like except the word itself.[1]

I remember once when I was doing my thesis and commuting between London and Oxford I evolved a variant on the completely conscious method. I had asked Sir George Joy[2] to leave objects out in his flat for me to guess while I was in Oxford. I used to wake up in the morning, think about what I wanted to do, consider the inconceivability of existence until I saw it, so to speak, and then let myself start to fall asleep again, watching my mind as if to catch the first start of a dream. Actually this produced rather distinct visual images, which of course made me come awake again, as soon as they happened.

Once I got a very clear visual image of a book – *Teach Yourself Malay*, it was, which was a book I had seen recently in the room of a friend in Somerville who had just come back from Borneo. So I came awake and thought about it. Obviously it couldn't actually be that book, but the question was whether it was a real book or not. I knew that in Sir George's flat there was an imitation wooden book, used as an ornament. So I put the question to myself whether it was a real book, or this wooden one, and fell asleep again. This time I got an image of an open book with the pages riffling over, as if in a wind. So I thought it must be a real book, and told Sir George so when I saw him next. Actually it had been his copy of *Omar Khayyám*, and he was disappointed that I hadn't got that. But one may note that the book-image I had seen had an Oriental association.

Of course I am not suggesting that this is evidence that ought to convince you. I very specifically did not undertake my personal experiments in order to add to the evidence, but to see what I could see about the psychology that went into it.

*

[1] Cf. William James, *The Principles of Psychology,* Dover Publications, New York, 1950, Vol. I, pp. 251–2.

[2] Sir George Joy, K.B.E., C.M.G., whose life and personality I refer to once or twice in this book, was a former Colonial Governor who assisted me in the foundation of the Institute and was for many years (until his death in 1975) a Trustee and Patron of it.

Should you wish to attempt psychokinesis, let me tell you how I think it is done. (The conditions are, however, you will observe, almost prohibitive.)

Any modern philosopher would mock an assertion that one thought one knew how something was done without ever having done it; however, I thought I knew the same about ESP before I found an opportunity of approximating sufficiently to the required conditions. The reason I attempted ESP but not PK was that the approximation is, in the former case, easier.

Part of the problem with ESP is that it is necessary to remove any sense of importance from what you are doing. It is difficult not to be aware that it is at variance with accepted theory, difficult not to feel that if you succeed you are proving that a new factor has to be taken into account. Part of what made it relatively easy was that, in a way, I found PK more obviously exciting from a scientific point of view, so I could feel that in attempting ESP I was only attempting a rather dull poor relation. And, by the time I attempted it, I was aware that there was actually rather a lot of evidence and I knew rather a lot of people who thought they had experienced it. This, while not conclusive, certainly helped to induce a feeling that the question of proving it wasn't what one was, at the moment, concerned with.

Of course these considerations were not fundamental enough, but certainly made it easier. It was necessary to try, but with the feeling that failure would be absolutely unimportant. Really what I depended on was the perception that since existence existed everything was so surprising anyway that it made very little difference to the totality of the surprisingness whether or not ESP was something that had to be taken into scientific account.

Now to attempt PK you would have, in the same way, to feel that what you were doing was of no significance. It is possible to be so astonished at being in a state of existence that it would seem to you no addition to the astonishingness of the situation if (say) a little silver paper knife picked itself up and floated gently across the room, but you would have to be in a state of rather intense astonishment.

It is not, in the first place, easy to get into a state which is intense and continuous enough for the purpose, and even if you do, there are drawbacks. I have referred before to a kind of decision-making psychological position. I am rather under the impression that a continuously realistic perception of the uncertainty of the situation in which one is is only possible in a certain rather highly evolved form of the decision-making position.

This effectively rules out all normal motivation. The various forms of the decision-making position are accompanied by an increasing impersonality of motivation. (I think impersonality is the nearest word, and conveys something about it, but it could be misleading.)

So that in a psychological state in which psychokinesis is an obvious possibility, you have no motivation to do it, or at any rate no predictable motivation. You could do it all right, if it happened to be what seemed like the thing to be done. But you do not have any vestige of a desire to prove this.

Of course, from a scientific point of view, this seems a bit awkward. But it does not have to be totally insoluble. I did find it possible to score highly at ESP by approximating to the ideal psychological conditions.[1] In the optimum state more stringent motivational considerations would have applied (and, very likely, if they could have been satisfied, I would have scored higher). Even in a less than optimal state the motivational restrictions were considerable, but they did not amount to impossibility.

But the approximation to the ideal psychological conditions, though it need not be perfect, must be good enough. If you want to make a tea-cup lift itself up in the air, you must somehow or another convince yourself that you won't be at all shocked or surprised if it does. (I recommend starting with small objects. Rationally or not, there is little doubt that the associated incredulity is less in the case of things that one can imagine oneself picking up quite easily by hand.)

[1] Cf. my book, *The Decline and Fall of Science*, Institute of Psychophysical Research, 1976, p. 87.

# CHAPTER 18

# Proving Things

An undergraduate physicist of Balliol became quite umbrageous on my pointing out that I didn't claim to have a theory of physics of my own, I was just critical of the goings on. He said quite sharply that he thought one would be expected to produce a complete theory of one's own, and prove it to be superior to any previous theory, before any criticism would be taken note of. Well that, I said, is indicative of a very unscientific and dogmatic outlook. 'Good *night*,' he said, and stormed off.

Yes, well, before I had any results in parapsychology there were those who told me that the reason I couldn't get support was that I hadn't produced results yet. Which I had only to do, and everyone would be falling over themselves with open-mindedness and generosity. Actually the non-support has become more total with everything that might have been supposed to stimulate it.

But this is an old game. When I was at school I was given to understand that I could have everything I wanted if I could only prove I was a genius. (Something like a new branch of mathematics would do.) Only I had to prove it while being treated as an average person, because if I was treated as a genius before I had proved I was one, that would make proving it too easy and it wouldn't be fair. Actually the result of not being treated as an exception was that I found it more and more difficult to work at all; while I still came top, my work became less and not more resoundingly brilliant, and this proved that my claim to require different conditions from other people was increasingly discredited.

Some time in the Kafkaesque arguments that I had at school

when I was fourteen I formulated my first axiom of psychology: You can't defeat motivation. However inconsistent I could make them appear, however clearly articulated my own statements, it wasn't the slightest good. Their attitudes were what they were, and they couldn't be changed.

Incidentally, it is interesting to note that I never did claim to be a genius. It was just that I found myself always forced into the position of someone whose requests for certain things were dependent on the proposition that they were a genius, and whose gratification in the requests was therefore dependent on their *proving* that they were.

It wasn't a thing I felt inclined to have an opinion about; in fact by psychological instinct I tended to think of myself as hard-working rather than brilliant; I wouldn't much care if I was the dullest research worker there was, just so long as I was doing research.

I was always aware that it wasn't at all a psychologically favourable position into which I was constantly forced; of having an opinion that I was fantastically brilliant and having to prove it in order to get the essentials of life. Actually I went on not having an opinion about my own ability, but I became aware that what might have been a psychological advantage was being turned against me, and my openness to belittling views of myself used to sell me impossibly destructive ones.

It wasn't until my first year at college that I decided I had better, after all, have an opinion about it. One would rather, of course, have been unassuming, been provided with the necessary conditions for working in the way one wanted (or at least in a way that was tolerable) and accepted the social opinion of oneself. But my chance of living like that had gone.

*

Laurence Olivier describes how, the night before opening in Richard III, he agonised in the expectation of giving the worst performance of his career.[1] Which is another example of what I

[1] *Daily Mail*, March 28, 1979, p. 32.

have said before; that success may very well be preceded by the strongest anticipation of failure. Hence, in order to succeed, it is a prerequisite that you do not get into a position in which the idea of failure cannot be entertained. (It may be supposed that Olivier did not think that failure in Richard III would be the irremediable end of his acting career.)

In the unhappiest stages of my education, if I tried to express my plight, I used to be told that if you worked steadily you would get a sense of mastery. But a sense of mastery was not something I had ever had. There was a way of taking the risk of failing that was exhilarating and perfectly right, as taking the School Certificate had been until I was stopped. There was a way of taking the risk that was harrowing but not unacceptable, which was what had happened until I got ahead of my age group. (I didn't suppose that any one failure would be the end of my prospects in life, but I anticipated hostility.)

But what you couldn't do was to maintain an unbroken confidence that you would succeed, any more than Olivier could, on the eve of Richard III, be smugly anticipating reviews as ecstatic as he actually received.

If you got into a position so psychologically adverse that you needed to maintain this sort of unbroken confidence, because failure was something you had to believe you could prevent, you had had it. (Or alternatively, I suppose, you are limited to exercising only those mental functions that can be made to work on a very conscious and mechanical level, without subconscious cooperation.)

Once my education had gone wrong I saw it as a virtually insoluble problem that I had been forced into this sort of position.

Another point from the Olivier interview was that he said he didn't think he was a great actor, because if he tried to put that belief into any of his performances, it wouldn't come out right. Well, again, of course, until my education went wrong, I had no inclination to believe anything about my ability; only to work as intensely as possible.

But what do you do once it has been made explicitly an issue, and apparently you can't start to think of doing anything you want in life until you've proved things about your ability to other people? So in my first year at college I decided that, after all, one couldn't postpone one's life until one had obtained other people's permission. And I don't have to prove I'm a genius, I thought, because after all I am. That felt right, and was; but it wasn't quite the final solution.

Later I saw that it was another of the risks that had to be taken; if you were a genius you couldn't get out of the possibility of failure. You might be good at it, or bad at it; they might very well make your life so difficult that you couldn't even get started on doing anything you wanted; it might very well be (which at the time seemed to me a very significant possibility) that my education had so jammed my psychology that I would never be able to think again. But there still wouldn't be any way you could turn yourself into a different sort of person, and you would have to go on, with ability or without it, trying to do the sort of things that apparently only geniuses were allowed to want to do.

# CHAPTER 19

# Risk-Taking (I)

If the human race likes to accept its own limitations, it likes even more to accept those of other people. So people find it charming when someone with a high I.Q. gets into difficulties; what motivation could there be to help them out of them. There isn't even any need to conceal their delight; it's taking them down a peg or two, and helping them learn they can't do everything.

As a matter of fact, I never supposed I could. My approach to life was precisely that which made self-satisfaction or even confidence of any normal kind least probable. This, of course, I think people knew, and it irritated them more than the obsession with social success for which, at times, they affected to mistake it.

I saw life as consisting of a constant battle with the limits of the possible; I was only interested in work as a way of functioning at the highest level of intensity. At its lowest and dullest I suppose my memory would still be measurably phenomenal; by concentrating so absolutely that you risked remembering nothing, it could be raised to an astonishing near-photographicness. And it was the same with one's other mental functions; they worked best if you took a risk on them. If you tried to work so slowly that you could check every step of what they were doing, they all but stopped working at all.

\*

Risk-taking is intrinsic to existential psychology; it is also intrinsic to mental activity, which is doubtless why the latter is so rare.

To take examinations fast is by no means the same thing as to take them slowly; quite different mental functions are used in the two cases.

Let us suppose that one wishes to take an examination in an unknown subject in a few days time. What is necessary is a total absence of preconceptions, a willingness to perceive all the possible implications of each idea at once, and all the interrelations of the ideas; and, finally, by the exercise of one's independent selectivity and judgement, to place all the facts in relation to those which are recognised as central. This process absolutely requires risk-taking; it is impossible to verbalise in a sequence all the mental operations that are taking place simultaneously; the more impossible the task appears the more essential it is to depend upon the autonomous classificatory powers of one's mind. Consciously, one has only to be aware of the intensity of focus upon one fact after another.

For example: when I was around twelve and was doing things fast I was in the habit of reading a theorem through once and memorising it as a single object – in much the same way that when I try to remember a teapot I do not recall, separately, that it has a spout, and that it has a lid, and that these things are in certain spatial relations to one another.

It is sometimes maintained that when people prepare for examinations within the last few days before them, they are failing to develop sufficient interrelations of ideas. The answer to this is evidently to frame your examinations in such a way that they test the formation of cognitive relationships, not to indulge in *a priori* assumptions about how rapidly such relationships may be formed.

Now I admit that not everyone (who has been brought up in a sane world) is able to perform the operations which I have described. There is also no guarantee that anyone who can perform the operations which I have described will be able to carry them out one hundred times more slowly – i.e. if given three hundred days instead of three within which to prepare for the same examination.

There is a certain speed at which it is possible to read a book so that you are primarily attending to the meaning of the book.

If, then, you are presented with the book at slower and slower rates – one sentence an hour, a few words thrice daily, one letter a day – what happens is not that you have progressively more time available in which to form more complex associations of ideas around the theme of the book, but that, after a time, you lose track of the theme completely. Mental activity, in fact, ceases. And if you were asked whether you were sure that you really understood the letter 'H' which was the letter for today, and whether you were sure that you had thoroughly learnt and understood the way in which it was related to the letter 'T' which came yesterday, you might find this difficult to answer.

This may appear an exaggerated example; but in fact it scarcely overstates the difference between the two levels of mental functioning, at least as I have experienced them. Education is geared to develop everyone's power to think on the T-H level. It is evident that other people can do this more successfully than I can. Virtually all modern intellectual productions must be regarded as exercises in making complicated and socially acceptable associations of words or symbols, without ever actually thinking.

There are, it must be admitted, drawbacks in the method of working fast which I have described. It leads to an ever-increasing intellectual voracity; to intensity, excitement and elation; to heightened physical and mental energy; to sudden perceptions and comprehensions; and, in particular, it must be admitted, it distinctly predisposes the subject to perceive the fact of existence.

# CHAPTER 20

# Risk-Taking (II)

Someone was trying to make me agree the other day that 'faith' might be a part of the psychology of ESP. In the sense of having confidence of success as the only possible outcome, it certainly isn't, at any rate so far as I am concerned. (Though some people seem to manage a psychological manoeuvre of this kind, e.g. Basil Shackleton, who was liable to assert, 'Next time I know I shall guess every card right', however often this failed to work out. Nevertheless he did score consistently above chance.)[1]

So far as I am concerned the only way to do it is to be able to envisage the possibility of total failure. This is related to the psychology of risk-taking in general.

It was when I was prevented from taking the School Certificate that I identified what I regarded as 'false security' and realised that people were trying to run my life in terms of it. It is not surprising that I never encountered much sympathy when I tried to explain this to people; most people's lives consist of nothing but just such 'false security' and the avoidance of the kind of risk-taking that I regarded as natural.

The arguments against my taking the School Certificate were all based on the idea that there might be a way of taking it, at a later age, which would make it certain that I would do well without either effort or the possibility of failure entering into the situation. (A few years later, I had come to regard it as ironic that these ways of running one's life so that strain and worry were entirely eliminated actually had the effect of exposing one

---

[1] Cf. S. G. Soal and F. Bateman, *Modern Experiments in Telepathy*, Faber, London, 1954.

to the most intolerable psychological torments, and making what one was trying to do all but impossible.)

As the disastrous years of my education began with a decision between the false security and the taking of a risk, so they ended with one; and this may perhaps further illustrate the psychological distinction.

You will recollect that my education ended with my being thrown out of college without a research scholarship, to fend for myself as best I could in the wilderness outside the official academic world. As I hadn't, to all intents and purposes, got a degree the obvious thing was to set about getting one. Originally I had hoped society would pay me for doing research in theoretical physics; I saw now that modern research in physics was being done in a way that didn't suit me much. So to finance myself in doing it my own way I needed a qualification that would enable me to earn money by doing research or giving tutorials in something else. Of course there was still the possibility of taking a degree in physics and financing oneself by doing research in physics (their brand). But the snag with taking a degree in physics would be that one would continue to be stimulated into trains of thought about it, as one had been while studying it as part of a maths degree, and it was essential, if one did decide to go on with getting a qualification, that one should postpone autonomous mental activities into the future. This would be easier if one were not constantly being reminded of the salient paradoxes which so evidently required thought.

The alternative was that one accepted that the qualification-getting time of one's life was over, although one hadn't got a qualification and would have to go through life without one. One had arrived at the time for doing research, so one had better aim as directly as possible at doing it. But there was no easy way of doing this, and this approach, as much as the other, required the postponement of life into the future, as I was sure that my autonomous trains of thought would be forcibly suppressed by any non-academic method of earning a living, even part-time. Still, it was more direct, even though it meant placing one's reliance wholly on such unforeseeable support and unlikely chances as might be found for someone founding an academic institute for themselves in the wilderness.

However, there was a considerable abandonment of security in deciding to make no further attempt to get a qualification. It would, after all, be so easy, if it were not for the matter of supporting oneself while one did it. (Society only supports you, I reflected ironically, to do things on condition that it can arrange them so that they are quite impossible — at any rate, if you are somebody like me.) My awareness of the psychological pitfalls to avoid was colossal; come to that, of course, I had always had a strong sense of the conditions and situations that suited me. What I hadn't known, and wouldn't have found out without the cooperation of the human race, was how bad you could get to feel, and how unfunctional you could make yourself, if you violated your psychological inclinations as brutally as possible.

Without a qualification I would have no social identity unless and until, doing my research in the wilderness, if indeed I ever got into a position to do it, in some unforeseeable future I should be re-admitted to social acceptance as an academic.

It was symptomatic of the isolation in which I already was that I discussed with nobody the plans I formulated and considered for taking a degree at the thirteenth hour, nor did anyone raise the matter with me. This may be contrasted with the constant pressure to which I was exposed when people wanted to persuade me to decide against taking the School Certificate. Then a way had been open to me, and they burningly desired that I should not take it. Now no way was open and I had to choose between two virtually impassable routes; I suppose everyone was content and saw no need to talk to me.

*

The other day someone asked me how I reconciled a predilection for risk-taking with a tendency to cultivate material security, in the form of freehold houses and investments selected for their resistance to recession and inflation. In fact what is in question is psychological risk-taking, and this only interests me

106

in the form of intellectual intensity, which can only be cultivated by being sufficiently free from distraction to devote a good
deal of time to intellectual input and by allowing the mind to
dwell upon paradoxical and possibly insoluble problems of
science and philosophy. (I always supposed it was the phenomenon of psychological risk-taking that Nietzsche really had in
mind when he said: Live dangerously. Erect your cities beside
Vesuvius. Live in a state of war.)

I don't myself see much attraction in taking physical risks; I
would find it too difficult to feel that there was much purpose in
doing so. However, those who can manage it may perhaps
experience similar psychological effects. Sir George Joy led a
very risky life in a conventionally adventurous way, and I think
he got out of it something like what Nietzsche had in mind.
Reference to a sort of risk-taking psychology can sometimes be
found in old-fashioned war poems, e.g.:

> *And when the burning moment breaks,*
> *And all things else are out of mind,*
> *And only Joy of Battle takes*
> *Him by the throat and makes him blind,*
>
> *Through joy and blindness he shall know,*
> *Not caring much to know, that still*
> *Nor lead nor steel shall reach him, so*
> *That it be not the Destined Will.*[1]

The phenomenon of risk-taking in the sense of leaving your
country and its allies largely undefended against attack, and
thus taking a chance on what it may cross the minds of your
enemies to do, is I believe something quite different.

[1] Julian Grenfell, 'Into Battle' (1915), quoted in full below, pp. 128–9.

# CHAPTER 21

# Private Incomes

It is interesting to note that if I had had even the smallest kind of private income, my education might have been saved from the ultimate disaster. Nothing could have given me any positive motivation to take a degree in maths at that stage of my life, but the threat of expulsion from academic life was altogether too great and had contributed a considerable degree of stress to my life for years. My mind was very active during the year just before my degree, as I found theoretical physics very stimulating, although the trains of thought it produced were unfortunately quite useless for degree purposes. Nevertheless, I liked my mental activities at that time, and the prospect of their brutal cessation was intolerable.

The stress in my life for years, and particularly at this final stage, would have been almost entirely eliminated if I had had at my disposal the means to ensure that I could continue to pursue my thoughts after my degree in even the smallest room.

This would obviously have reduced the loading against me in my constant struggles to induce my mind to pay attention to working for a degree. The distraction caused by interesting but extra-curricular trains of thought would not have been much less (though there was an element of urgency in them, as if they had to complete themselves as far as possible, since after my degree I could not be sure when I could again secure the conditions for thinking), but the nightmarishness caused by the insoluble horrors that might lie ahead would have been virtually absent. A state of horror and panic is extremely bad for doing maths, and even the maintenance of a state of resolution in face of uncharted difficulties takes more emotional energy than it may seem to. It is by no means the same thing as being in a position in which the future cannot, whatever the result of one's degree, present one with an extreme order of difficulty.

Perhaps people should regard providing their children with at least very small private incomes as the first essential in contributing to their success in life – even more important than paying for their education privately.

# CHAPTER 22

# Taking One's Chances

The most important issues in psychology are absent from all recognised psychological systems and, perhaps, even more conspicuously suppressed from the various mystical traditions, which should presumably be regarded as psychological traditions if they have any significance at all. So they are only to be found in literature, obliquely and fragmentarily referred to.

*Hamlet* has a sub-plot, or rather a subliminal plot. It is about somebody not taking a great chance. Chances don't present themselves often; it is difficult even, so to speak, to qualify for one, and no one tells you how it is done. But occasionally one knows, in a certain way, what one wants to do.

The loading on such situations is greater than anyone might suspect (at least in my experience). The consequences, positive or negative, lie beyond the scope of rational prediction. (Not that they are irrational, only unpredictable.) The only real reason for doing whatever it is is that you want to; it has a tendency to be open to all sorts of 'commonsense' objections, and to arouse storms of social opposition if persisted in. And since there is likely to be so much against it, no doubt it is fairly easy to convince yourself you don't really want to do it.

Once I was talked out of doing something I really wanted to do (viz. to take the School Certificate at short notice ahead of the age limit) and the consequences were more horrific than I could have imagined. On account of the total lack of agreement between me and those around me about how my life should be run, I stopped having any feeling of contact with my own criteria for living, and could not see how I would ever be able to get back to living in a way that felt right. Eventually it occurred to me, years later, that there was something I wanted to do, i.e.

to have two teeth out without an anaesthetic. It wasn't at all the sort of thing I would have expected, but undeniably it had that feeling about it. By this time it was perfectly clear to me that there was one sort of risk I would never take again; the risk of not doing something I really (in that way) wanted to. I had made a mistake about it once, and it was still not clear to me whether a lifetime was long enough to recover from it. I didn't expect anything particular to come of the thing about the teeth; it didn't seem to be of great significance. What I had thought of might be an interesting psychological trick; but of no great theoretical importance. And why try it now rather than some other time? There always might be something else . . . some other time . . . Socially it seemed unnecessary, perhaps grotesque. But I realised by now that not letting yourself be talked out of things was half the battle. The consequences were staggering and in the strictest sense unforeseeable.

I was astonished to find that the positive results of doing what you wanted could be more than commensurate with the negative results of not doing it.

*Hamlet* has a kind of nostalgia about it that scarcely goes with its alleged theme of avenging murder and incest. And Hamlet, in the early stages, has a kind of layered detachment that suggests someone open to incalculable possibilities. There is a change of tone, perhaps, where he concocts the scheme with the players. Possibly this corresponds to someone starting to say, 'Maybe I shall do what I see is to be done later on, but it *cannot be wrong* to do so-and-so *first*.' (First I must consult a social expert, bury my dead, etc.)

Henceforward he is less layered and increasingly the helpless victim of circumstance, as in effect he has chosen to be (as all choose to be who do not do what they really want).

And in the end you have this sense of something great that hasn't happened. It is right that the profoundest nostalgia of the human race should attach itself to such things; but how do they know, when the chance is so rarely taken?

\*

Once upon a time I had two teeth out without an anaesthetic (molars it was). There is no need to start feeling harrowed; it was very jolly.

When I got up to college, my psychology was in a parlous state. Therefore I took up psychology. I did not think much of psychology as a field of research, and I did this only as a matter of expediency. Later I came to think that psychology had, perhaps, rather more in the way of intellectual potentialities than I had thought at first. However, I regarded it as a tiresome detour, the object of which was to restore me to a state of functionality and relationship to my work.

I avoided reading any normal psychology or psychiatry; by which it should not be supposed that I was ever in a state of great *naïveté*. I had always had a way of picking up anybody's system of ideas from a page or two here and there in their books, and I had always had a tendency to pick up books. Furthermore, a number of people had devoted a great many manhours to grilling me with a view to changing my psychology, and I had quite seen what they were aiming at; both what they were really aiming at and what they would have professed.

However, from the start my psychological reflections were of some originality.

Around the end of my first year I had occasion to ask myself: 'How has it come about that I can't bear to look at a maths book for anything but the shortest possible time?' and from that derived the psychological principle that pain is always a matter of trying (for some reason) not to see what is there (i.e., in the initial case, trying not to see the associations of ideas provoked by the book). This became intrinsic to my methods of eliminating conflict.

Around the start of my third year it transpired that I had to have two teeth out. It occurred to me that there ought to be a psychological solution to physical pain; I was virtually convinced that there must be from odd anecdotes I had heard, and reflected on the matter. (That is to say: I applied the most violent possible method to extracting the information from my subconscious by heightening the emotional intolerability of the situation to a point at which something had to give way.)

Actually the solution is quite simple. The problem is not the pain but the reaction to the pain, which is automatic and strong and with which something has to be done. If it becomes formulated as wanting to stop the pain, there is no way it can set about doing this that will not lead to conflict. A desire to fight the dentist would have to be opposed; a desire to set up a counter-irritant might have partial success, but only partial; presumably people who are screaming loudly are, to some extent, reducing their suffering.

What then can the aggressive drive produced by the pain go into with any chance of success? Well, of course, if it goes into wanting the pain to continue, trying as it were to produce it, it will succeed; the pain will become an assertion of one's own will and there will be no conflict. (Conflict arising always from the fact that a specific violation of one's will is seen as a proof of finiteness, or rather has to be not seen as it, and hence the conflict.)

This worked quite well while the dentist drilled a few holes and then he started talking about what anaesthetic I would have when I came the next time to have the teeth out. I broke the news to him that I wouldn't have any and he was going to have the opportunity of assisting in an interesting scientific experiment. Fortunately for me he was young and impressionable; it could have made life very difficult if he had refused. As it was he confined himself to telling me horror stories to convince me that having teeth out was an awfully drastic business. It only made me feel more interested to find out whether my method would work.

I thought that the start would be crucial; you couldn't start to aggress at the pain until you got the reaction to the pain, and until it started you wouldn't know exactly what the complex of sensations was going to be like, with any possibly conflict-arousing associations. But if you lost control of the situation at the outset it might be awfully difficult to regain it. So you had to be sure to bat the reaction straight back as an aggression at the pain just as soon as there was a reaction at all.

Actually, that was how it was. The first sensations; the reaction, and then as you aimed it back at the pain, it was exactly as if the pain receded to a convenient and comfortable distance. Of course, in retrospect one could see that this effect of recession was actually just a change in the emotional quality of the pain, but it was a very striking one. It was only from the first split-second of sensation that one could imagine afterwards how different the experience might have been, because once the situation was set up it stayed like that. Of course I watched it most carefully in case anything started to get out of place and needed to be reasserted; but actually it was a piece of cake.

The point is that if you eliminate the emotional conflict from pain it is just sensation, and its variations in quality and intensity are interesting in just as neutral a way as the variations in visual sensation.

*Postscript*. The above exposition is complete so far as it goes. However, a lot of collateral and subsidiary analysis went into it and I wouldn't recommend anyone to try using the method on anything serious unless they had used it on fairly trivial things first, and then not without circumspection.

*

The human race has, as one can hardly fail to know, this thing about accepting its limitations.

When I was describing somewhat briefly to a visitor who described herself as a Creative Psychologist how to have teeth out without an anaesthetic, she murmured, as if endorsing what I said, 'One must accept one's limitations.' That was rather clever of her, in a way, because it is so precisely what it doesn't depend on. (As Henry James might have said.)

In fact one might say that it is all this accepting of limitations that makes pain what it (usually) is; as well as making human psychology in general what it is, with its belief in society, desire to restrict other people, and so forth.

It may be possible to apply the thing about pain sufficiently well without relating it to its most fundamental principles (and

I think, at any rate to some extent, it is, as various people have told me they applied it to sundry minor situations). But *au fond*, it must be admitted, it depends upon the fact that any conflict can be eliminated so long as you do not accept your limitations. So long, that is, as you do not prevent the reaction to finiteness from turning into the drive to infinity (which will do as a name for the extremely abstract central drive of psychology, which becomes more difficult to define as it becomes more obvious).

# CHAPTER 23

# The Belief in Society

During my first year at college I gave up believing in society.

Of course, I had never believed in it a great deal, by the prevailing standards. I was very good at the total uncertainty when I was twelve and when I was thirteen the writers I was most aware of were all characterised by a sort of analytical detachment towards human affairs: Wells, Shaw, Voltaire, Oscar Wilde, Herbert Spencer.

In fact this detachment of outlook, although I scarcely advertised it, had ostensibly been one of the reasons why I had been so enormously disapproved of. People had been intensely alert to any failure on my part to evince an infinitely uncritical devotion to social values, any lack of sentimental attachment to school hat badges, any lack of reverence towards the human mating and breeding cycle, and so forth. Even if I tried to say the socially acceptable thing, it wasn't accepted, so I gave up trying. It was one of the mild peculiarities of my life that, while I was always being exhorted to stop studying and *talk* to people, I couldn't actually open my mouth without the environment exploding around me.

And yet, although I had always (at any rate from the age of eleven) practised the constant detection and analysis of unanalysed assumptions, I found when it came to it that there was still some sense in which one preserved a residual belief in society as a source of significance.

By this time, of course, my psychology was in no sense a going concern. I had been prevented, more or less forcibly, from doing what I wanted to do when I wanted to do it, and a number of people had worked over my psychology with a view to reforming it. At least ostensibly. I found it difficult to think that the motivation had really been anything but the production of the maximum quantity of conflicts and blockages, but whether that was so or not, the conflicts and blockages had certainly resulted.

So they had to be undone; and I saw that by now this residual desire to believe in the value of social approval was doing me no good at all. It is difficult to say quite what this final abstract minimum consisted of, but I saw quite distinctly, although with misgiving, that it would be possible to break it. Only I thought that things would never be the same again. Surely it was innocent enough to want to get something out of social success, if you could ever manage to get it. At this time it seemed a possibility of the most infinite remoteness that I could ever, in any case, become successful at anything on social terms again, so it was perhaps strange that one should still want to preserve the ability to feel that it was significant if one did.

And intensity, I thought, would always be less. If intellectual intensity had to be totally divorced from any feeling of the glamour of social recognition, wouldn't a dimension of drama be lacking from life, and wouldn't the intensity be always less than it might have been?

But I saw that I didn't have much choice; the question was to survive at all, and it might very well be the case that half-cock intensity was all I would get back, but at present I hadn't any.

One way in which society evidently wouldn't be able to give one anything any more was that one wouldn't be able to accept any compliments uncritically; one would always see them as the product of a certain mind and a certain psychology.

And that is perhaps an indication why the belief in society is so potent a force in psychology; because the retention of it, in however attenuated or subconscious a form, prevents one from knowing one's own mind.

*

Possibly one should emphasise how extreme a procedure it seemed at the time to adopt a position that would deprive any possible social approval of its glamour. (Some of my earliest psychological manoeuvres have now become so much second nature or else irrelevant that it is difficult to remember that they should still be stated.)

Supposing the manoeuvres I performed before I got to be able to score highly at ESP to be of relevance to the psychodynamics of that function, this is probably a fairly crucial one, and would go far to account for the rarity of the phenomenon. Most people obviously don't anticipate positions of complete isolation and opposition, but rely on maintaining some sort of a semblance of alignment with social agreement.

But my position had got to be too desperate. There is a sort of feeling that you mustn't allow yourself to understand things about yourself until you have got other people to agree to understand them that way; I had to be free to understand what I could understand even if no one else would agree to it at all.

It did have rather the feeling of amputating a mangled limb. There was nothing wrong with the limb originally, I thought; why shouldn't social approval, if one could get it, add an extra spice to what you got anyway out of doing things as totally as possible. If things had worked out otherwise, it might have been possible to keep it. But now it would have to go.

*

The belief in society prevents one from knowing one's own mind. To know one's own mind is a very technical matter, and not much practised.

In the simplest way this can be seen in the well-known fact that flattery can be used to blind the victim to the motivation of the flatterer. In order to have significance conferred upon him, he stops using his own judgement.

Cf. Aesop's fable in which the fox induces the crow to relinquish his hold on the highly desirable cheese by professing an admiration of his singing voice.

Of course in so simple a case what the victim is prevented from thinking is fairly obvious and accessible even to his own conscious inspection if he devotes a little thought to it. But the desire to derive significance from social approval can be (and of course usually is) present in a way which has enormous subconscious implications, and the trains of thought which the possessor is being inhibited from having are not at all obvious, nor the psychological positions which he is being prevented from occupying.

To take a slightly more sophisticated example: most people, if they read relativity or learn quantum theory, are motivated, more or less consciously, by a desire to obtain social approval (even if only their own social approval, so to speak) by demonstrating their ability to understand these socially statusful things. This produces the most amazing imperviousness to meaningless and inconsistent statements in what they are reading, and they do not give a thought to the motivation of the people who wrote it.

Already, in such a case, it is not too obvious what an inhibited person is being prevented from thinking.

*

But of course to a certain extent the examples I have given are misleading, because they suggest that what principally holds the human psychosis in place is the desire for personal glory, in however abstract a sense, and the human race is quite willing to recognise the existence of this motive.

So long as the belief in society actually is only held in place by the desire for personal significance it is probably much less stable than in its more characteristic form, in which it is held in place by the desire to diminish the significance of others. This motive is, one must believe, extremely powerful.

Reading a book on psychological testing recently I came across a passage where the author was discussing people's dislike of such tests. Paraphrasing roughly, the author said: No doubt people do not altogether like having their abilities and attributes quantified and placed on a numerical scale in relation to other people's, but these tests are very useful and people should be induced to accept them. After all, nobody is good at everything. One should always reflect that however great the abilities of some other person may be, there is sure to be something he is bad at.

One really might wonder how on earth that was supposed to be relevant, if one were not already acquainted with the syndrome.

A child psychologist recently sounded off to the effect that children like bionic men and women because fantasies of magic are consoling to their sense of weakness, lack of control of their destiny, etc. If adults are supposed not to need consolations of this kind because they feel their size and strength is quite sufficient, they must just be less realistic than children. Or, more probably, they have acquired that different form of consolation which consists of belittling one another.

*

But, of course, you may very well say that one has to believe in society to some extent. After all, one has to live; one has to do something; being efficient and moralised is an agreeable state and one must give oneself some incentive. While fully aware of the similarity between the human race and an ant-hill spinning in space, what harm can it do to ascribe a certain weighting to the goings-on of society, the consensus of current opinion, and so forth. And this is very reasonable; I thought so once myself.

However, it is a position which contains certain weaknesses, both actual and potential. The actual weaknesses may pass unnoticed indefinitely, since if all goes well such an outlook is not incompatible with even quite a high degree of knowing one's mind. But all may not go well; society may exploit the situation so as to leave you a space altogether too small to live in, as if wishing to force a total capitulation.

One of the weaknesses in the psychological position of almost everybody is the assumption that there will always be a way of avoiding complete social disapproval; that they will never have to find themselves in a minority of one.

There were dangerous elements in the psychology of Victorian intellectuals. Probably you have never read the poems of

Myers; however, he was a minor poet, and his best-known poem contains the following:

> Whoso has felt the Spirit of the Highest
> Cannot confound nor doubt Him nor deny:
> Yea with one voice, o world, tho' thou deniest,
> Stand thou on that side, for on this am I.
>
> Rather the earth shall doubt when her retrieving
> Pours in the rain and rushes from the sod,
> Rather than he for whom the great conceiving
> Stirs in his soul to quicken into God.
>
> Ay, tho' thou then shouldst strike him from his glory
> Blind and tormented, maddened and alone,
> Even on the cross would he maintain his story,
> Yes and in hell would whisper, I have known.[1]

The idea of an individual standing alone against the world was a very dangerous one; the human race is quite right to regard it so.

[1] From *Saint Paul* by F. W. H. Myers, included in *Poems*, Macmillan, London, 1870.

# CHAPTER 24

# Centralisation (I)

I need to introduce a piece of terminology.

There is a kind of being identified with one's life that I came to call centralisation. In many of its forms it clearly involves everything being related to some central factor.

At first I found it very difficult to define. When I had it most nearly in focus it seemed to me that it was something to do with accepting the responsibility for one's life, something to do with feeling identified with it, and something to do with a sense of purpose. If you took the point of intersection of those three things, as it were, all in the most abstract sense, maybe you had it.

But I found it, with my life as it was when I first came up to university, terribly difficult to get back into this position.

For one thing, there was now no congruity between the social view of one's position and one's own, so one felt as if one had to re-establish this before one could feel identified with one's life again. At first sight a life in which one had to be entirely opposed to the social view of oneself seemed to be something one disowned. So (and of course this was what people encouraged one to regard as the only way of tackling the problem) if one could force oneself to work, however negative work had become, maybe one would start in patches to get some sort of positive feedback, and gradually the positive feedback system could be re-established. But to turn a negative feedback system into a positive one is a very difficult matter; at least, I found it so.

So then I came to think: it is no use thinking that one will be identified with one's life when one no longer has to consider the possibility of the ultimate crunch between oneself and society, because all one's energy is engaged at keeping at bay the awareness of this possible crunch. So suppose it can't be averted; if they tell one one isn't good enough to do research, *will* one believe it?

Of course I had been brought up to know that social outcasts who believed they had great abilities were the ultimate objects of derision and contempt; and it is easy to persuade intelligent and idealistic people that it is virtuous and objective to believe criticisms of themselves expressed by persons in authoritative positions.

So I found the conclusion horrifying. But if that is how it is, that is how it is, I thought, and there is no use pretending it is otherwise. You will certainly go on doing research, or trying to find a way to do research, however bad they tell you you are, and however bad you actually may be.

And, furthermore, you must give up any hope that any of them will ever come to understand anything about you, because trying to think that the things they say and think about you bear any relation to anything that is actually the case is only taking up energy and dragging you into impossible positions.

Curiously enough, this seemed like a great loss; as if I was jettisoning for ever any possibility that any social recognition could ever mean anything to me. Which, actually, I was, because to get anything out of social praise you have to stop thinking for yourself and think of the source of the praise as 'a professor' or 'a reviewer' and hence at least slightly numinous. However, later the loss came to seem not very great.

To be centralised you have at least to accept the possibility of finding yourself alone against the world; this is logical in a way, because to know your own mind you evidently have to let it tell you things, and you do not know what it will tell you until it does. So it is impossible to be sure that it will not tell you that everybody else is up a gum-tree.

Years later I started to collect literary examples of centralisation. There aren't many; the human race doesn't go in for it that much. But the few that recognisably express it do tend to have the sense of being (at least potentially — and one might notice that; the sense of being actually and definitely so is not necessarily the same thing at all) entirely alone against the world.

Consider, for example, the following: the familiar *Invictus* (though not so familiar, it seems, to people who have been to school recently).

### INVICTUS

*Out of the night that covers me,*
*Black as the Pit from pole to pole,*
*I thank whatever gods may be*
*For my unconquerable soul.*

*In the fell clutch of circumstance*
*I have not winced nor cried aloud.*
*Under the bludgeonings of chance*
*My head is bloody, but unbowed.*

*Beyond this place of wrath and tears*
*Looms but the Horror of the shade,*
*And yet the menace of the years*
*Finds, and shall find, me unafraid.*

*It matters not how strait the gate,*
*How charged with punishments the scroll,*
*I am the master of my fate:*
*I am the captain of my soul.*

*W. E. HENLEY*

It may be noticed that there is no way centralisation can be made compatible with the dependence on social guide-lines required of modern man. There is no such thing as a free lunch, and if the human race offers you a mess of pottage it is necessary to think carefully whether perhaps the price being required of you is your birthright.

# CHAPTER 25

# Centralisation (II)

Centralisation depends (among other things) on an analytical attitude towards what is under one's control, and what is not. You might like to compare the following poem by myself, written quite early on when I was at college, with the stanzas which have already been quoted from Myers on page 121. They are both quite accurate descriptions of centralised psychological states, and you will observe that they both have a somewhat extreme awareness of the extent to which external (and even internal) circumstances may become disadvantageous.

> *I will desire with no compromise;*
> *I will set my will against the most high;*
> *I will fight these sordid things so long as need be;*
> *And I will never lose courage*
> *Nor consent to die.*

Observe the fetching precision of the last line. It always seemed to me that my education was really about my total destruction. Realistically, I could not be sure that I would not be destroyed; however, it occurred to me that I would never agree to it.

Myers's poem is interesting in that it envisages the possibility of being in total opposition to social agreement. This is something which I do not think people envisage very often. One may be centralised after a fashion without having envisaged this possibility, but I do not think it would be possible to be continuously aware of existence without having done so.

It is not necessary, of course, to hold an opinion to the effect that other human beings are hostile to oneself to perceive that one could not prevent them from acting in such a manner as to render one's life superlatively uncomfortable. And then, of course, circumstances can become adverse without any intervention on the part of the human race.

As usual, all that is really necessary is the perception of the possibilities of the situation. The Gnostic religion, or some versions of it, appear to regard the world as evil or demonic. This is an opinion, and it is not necessary to hold opinions. (In fact, it is necessary not to hold them.)

*

A sense of responsibility (in my sense) is related to a somewhat analytical attitude to what, in fact, one is being responsible *for*.

Here, the transition from normal to centralised psychology may appear paradoxical. It is only by an extreme narrowing down of one's area of responsibility that there is any possibility of accepting the responsibility for perceiving the existential situation as it actually is, and the shocking enormity of the position in which one finds oneself.

People normally regard as their 'area of responsibility' a great many things about their own psychology which are not under their own control, other people's psychology, and even the state of affairs in the world. For example, people are encouraged to feel responsible (in this sense) for the fact that not everyone in the world is well fed.

To be more autobiographical, I was encouraged (in fact positively brainwashed) to believe that I ought to feel *responsible* for not being able to work under conditions which were most forcibly, and most obviously against my will, imposed on me by other people.

It is actually necessary to realise what is not under one's control before there is any possibility of responsibility (in the existential sense).

*

Centralised psychology, even at the elementary level, does not lend itself to the toe-dipping approach. It will be observed that, of the three examples already given, all contain an element of commitment *in perpetuity* to a given attitude. (I regret the word commitment, which has been invested with overtones I do not mean; however, one has to make the best one can of the language.)

You may of course think it is very unfair and unreasonable of centralised psychology to make itself so inaccessible to sensible and judicious sampling procedures; however, curiously enough, that is the way it is.

# CHAPTER 26

# Centralisation (III)

Several variants of centralisation are possible, but as it is not exactly the done thing to be centralised most of the literary examples are transitory and partial ones. By now, I have given two such examples: Henley and Myers. To these we may add Julian Grenfell's poem 'Into Battle':

> The naked earth is warm with Spring,
> And with green grass and bursting trees
> Leans to the sun's gaze glorying
> And quivers in the sunny breeze;
>
> And life is Colour and Warmth and Light,
> And a striving evermore for these;
> And he is dead who will not fight,
> And who dies fighting has increase.
>
> The fighting man shall from the sun
> Take warmth, and life from the glowing earth;
> Speed with the light-foot winds to run,
> And with the trees to newer birth;
> And find, when fighting shall be done,
> Great rest, and fullness after death.
>
> All the bright company of Heaven
> Hold him in their high comradeship,
> The Dog-star, and the Sisters Seven,
> Orion's Belt and sworded hip.
>
> The woodland trees that stand together,
> They stand to him each one a friend;
> They gently speak in the windy weather;
> They guide to valley and ridge's end.

*The kestrel hovering by day,*
*And the little owls that call by night,*
*Bid him be swift and keen as they,*
*As keen of ear, as swift of sight.*

*The blackbird sings to him, 'Brother, brother,*
*If this be the last song you shall sing*
*Sing well, for you may not sing another;*
*Brother, sing.'*

*In dreary doubtful waiting hours,*
*Before the brazen frenzy starts,*
*The horses show him nobler powers; —*
*O patient eyes, courageous hearts!*

*And when the burning moment breaks,*
*And all things else are out of mind,*
*And only Joy of Battle takes*
*Him by the throat and makes him blind,*

*Through joy and blindness he shall know,*
*Not caring much to know, that still*
*Nor lead nor steel shall reach him, so*
*That it be not the Destined Will.*

*The thundering line of battle stands,*
*And in the air Death moans and sings;*
*But Day shall clasp him with strong hands,*
*And Night shall fold him in soft wings.*

JULIAN GRENFELL

(Keats's version of centralisation is:

> *. . . to bear all naked truths,*
> *And to envisage circumstance, all calm,*
> *That is the top of sovereignty.*

*(Hyperion)*

'All calm' spoils that.)

The last verse but one of Julian Grenfell is particularly good; the certainty and detachment from certainty characteristic of existential psychology – to be contrasted with the uncertainty and fixation on security and familiarity characteristic of sanity. This is what Nietzsche meant by 'living dangerously'. You don't need a war to help you do it, of course. You can live dangerously in bed at night, if you think a few realistic thoughts.

Carlyle had a centralised reaction once: from depression to a kind of assertion in the face of death, excluding fear. From this he derived an idea of a centralised personality (though not a very clear one) and spent a lot of time writing about heroes and great men.

This is how he describes the experience which he regarded as a crucial turning-point in his life:

'Full of such humour, and perhaps the miserablest man in the whole French Capital or Suburbs, was I, one sultry Dog-day, after much perambulation, toiling along the dirty little *Rue Saint-Thomas de l'Enfer,* among civic rubbish enough, in a close atmosphere, and over pavements hot as Nebuchadnezzar's Furnace; whereby doubtless my spirits were little cheered; when, all at once, there rose a Thought in me, and I asked myself: "What *art* thou afraid of? Wherefore, like a coward, dost thou forever pip and whimper, and go cowering and trembling? Despicable biped! what is the sum-total of the worst that lies before thee? Death? Well, Death; and say the pangs of Tophet too, and all that the Devil and Man may, will or can do against thee! Hast thou not a heart; canst thou not suffer whatsoever it be; and, as a Child of Freedom, though outcast, trample Tophet itself under thy feet, while it consumes thee? Let it come, then; I will meet it and defy it!" And as I so thought, there rushed like a stream of fire over my whole soul; and I shook base Fear away from me forever. I was strong, of unknown strength; a spirit, almost a god. Ever from that time, the temper of my misery was changed: not Fear or whining Sorrow was it, but Indignation and grim fire-eyed Defiance.'[1]

Centralisation can have different central terms. E.g. Milton was probably centralised on the fact that he was a very important person and going to do something very significant; and he would have tried not to do anything incompatible with that.

[1] Thomas Carlyle, *Sartor resartus*, Dent, London, 1908, p. 127. It is generally accepted that the passage quoted, although not directly autobiographical, reflects an experience of Carlyle's own.

This is, in a way, feeling responsible for doing the best possible thing with your life. Milton does understand something about centralisation; incidentally, he makes his people express themselves in a centralised way even when the attitudes they are expressing are not centralised ones.

# CHAPTER 27

# Centralisation (IV)

So far I have omitted to describe the state of risk-taking psychology in which I was approaching the School Certificate examination, until prevented. In retrospect I realise that it had many of the characteristics of what I should now regard as quite a highly evolved state of centralisation.

From the time I first went to the convent grammar school until I was first put up a year, my life was grim but, technically, centralised. I.e. I lived in considerable intensity and was very identified with what I was doing.

When I first got ahead of my age group my life became altogether more joyful, and having to make up a year's work in various subjects at a moment's notice made me aware that one possessed rather high-powered psychological machinery which only came into operation when it was needed; i.e. when it was presented with something to do that appeared marginally impossible – at any rate, somewhat beyond the scope of what one could consciously see how to do, using the dullest and most foreseeable part of one's mind. It seemed to me, of course, that having realised this one should continue to work in such a way as to keep the more interesting levels of one's mind operative, which meant hard enough and fast enough. (Hence, of course, the insoluble future conflicts of my education. My desire for quantities of work sufficiently challenging to ensure wakefulness could always be stigmatised as greed, selfishness, lack of balance, lack of social adjustment, ambition and what-have-you. However, this lay in the future. The first, but crucial, conflict over the School Certificate is what we are at present concerned with.)

The suggestion that I might take the School Certificate

straight away at short notice, in order not to be held up by the age limit, could not have come at a better time so far as I was concerned. I had the sense of newly-discovered mental faculties, without yet much experience of using them. Other people might be under the impression that I should be fainting with weariness after rather rapidly coming top of a new form, but that was not the way it felt. If anything, I felt I had been being quite frivolous and after such a jolly holiday a little serious work would be precisely right.

So I set about preparing for this School Certificate, and as I did so all the high-powered machinery of which I had started to become aware seemed to emerge and fuse itself into an engine of enormous energy, functioning with the most beautifully coordinated exactitude and inexorably directed towards arriving at the date of the examination with a total and precise grasp of every relevant fact. But this was partly where the risk-taking came in; although perhaps I half suspected at the time that this would be the outcome, and suspected it even more clearly in retrospect, I was actually concentrating so absolutely that predictions as to the outcome could scarcely cross one's mind.

One of the pieces of mental machinery that only appeared to become operative when they were provided with something sufficiently demanding to do was a kind of faculty for structuring new sets of ideas, which one became aware of when one had to learn a new subject at rather short notice. It seemed to select the central factors and throw everything into a coherent structure around them with an assurance that never seemed quite accountable in terms of the inferences one could see that one had been able to make. I am not saying that there was anything preternatural about it, but the process took place in a way that was slightly surprising, so that one was carried along by a sort of curiosity to discover whether the structure that had so far been put together would really turn out to be justified when one had fuller information. Someone who knew me once said that when I was picking up some new set of ideas it was rather as if I knew in advance how they were going to fit together, or that I could put any of them in place before I knew the others; rather as if someone were to start building a house by throwing a window up into the air and then assembling the rest of the structure around it as it came to hand.

Be that as it may, on this occasion I had a feeling that my mind had taken a terrifically strong grasp on the whole situation, and had it all worked out exactly what needed to be done, and in what order, in order to arrive with the optimum preparation at the precise day of the exams. And one was carried along by the same kind of half-explicit curiosity to find out whether it really had.

As I say, the state I was living in had many of the characteristics of centralised psychology. Obviously there was a terrifically clear central drive, combined with that sense of extraordinary rightness and obviousness, and of release from conflict.

Of course it seemed to me that I had just found out the right and natural way of living. It seemed a tremendous relief after the strain of living previously in a way so unnecessarily stressful.

*

C.S. Lewis describes a certain kind of nostalgia or longing the experience of which is itself an object of desire.

> The experience is one of intense longing. It is distinguished from other longings by two things. In the first place, though the sense of want is acute and even painful, yet the mere wanting is felt to be somehow a delight. Other desires are felt as pleasures only if satisfaction is expected in the near future: hunger is pleasant only while we know (or believe) that we are soon going to eat. But this desire, even when there is no hope of possible satisfaction, continues to be prized, and even to be preferred to anything else in the world, by those who have once felt it. This hunger is better than any other fullness; this poverty better than all other wealth. And thus it comes about, that if the desire is long absent, it may itself be desired, and that new desiring becomes a new instance of the original desire, though the subject may not at once recognise the fact and thus cries out for his lost youth of soul at the very moment in which he is being rejuvenated. This sounds complicated, but it is simple when we live it. 'Oh to feel as I did then!' we cry; not noticing that even while we say the words the very feelings whose loss we lament is rising again in all its old bitter-sweetness. For this sweet Desire cuts across our ordinary distinc-

tions between wanting and having. To have it is, by definition, a want: to want it, we find, is to have it.

In the second place, there is a peculiar mystery about the *object* of this Desire. Inexperienced people (and inattention leaves some inexperienced all their lives) suppose, when they feel it, that they know what they are desiring. Thus if it comes to a child while he is looking at a far off hillside he at once thinks 'if only I were there'; if it comes when he is remembering some event in the past, he thinks 'if only I could go back to those days'. If it comes (a little later) while he is reading a 'romantic' tale or poem of 'perilous seas and faerie lands forlorn', he thinks he is wishing that such places really existed and that he could reach them. If it comes (later still) in a context with erotic suggestions he believes he is desiring the perfect beloved. If he falls upon literature (like Maeterlinck or the early Yeats) which treats of spirits and the like with some show of serious belief, he may think that he is hankering for real magic and occultism. When it darts out upon him from his studies in history or science, he may confuse it with the intellectual craving for knowledge.[1]

I don't think C. S. Lewis had much understanding of centralised psychology, although sometimes the psychological points he makes are closer to being relevant than one might expect. However, one may at any rate say that this sort of longing is characteristic of centralised psychology, though he describes it only as a fleeting phenomenon.

There is a very strong drive to return to any distinctively centralised state of psychology. If the drive is frustrated, considerable disorientation and depression can result. This may account for the downfall of a certain number of high I.Q. failures (though I am far from assuming that many of them are much like myself). Maybe also for the psychological disorientation of ex-war heroes; and, in short, anyone who has ever found themselves doing something in an intensely purposeful kind of way.

It is, I think, almost a universal characteristic of fairly highly evolved centralised psychology that there is a strongly optimistic expectancy, although this may be more or less implicit. This is why Wagner's music tends to remind one of centralised

[1] C. S. Lewis, *The Pilgrim's Regress*, Collins (Fount Paperback), London, 1977, pp. 12–13.

states. To return to the specific example, that of my psychology before I was stopped from taking this exam: the expectancy could be taken as relating to some new and interesting perception of a relationship in one's work that might strike one at any moment, or to an elation even more intense that might occur if one continued to concentrate hard enough on what one was doing, or to the concealed anticipation of extraordinary success in the exam. In retrospect I could hardly doubt that, if I hadn't been prevented, I would have got somewhere near to a hundred per cent in everything, although so long as I was still working for the exam and thought I would take it, I was far too concentrated to have any opinion of that kind about the outcome.

Of course, the effect of breaking off such a process in midstream was shattering. What had one lost? A few months of elated concentration; the triumphant climax of outstanding success when the results were known. Freedom to continue working for more advanced exams without being hindered by the age limit. That was certainly considerable enough. But considerable though it was, was it even so really all that one had lost? Could one be sure that something incalculably tremendous might not have occurred to one?

I now think that the passionate expectancy of centralised psychology is not illusory. To live in any centralised state is to be liable to find oneself in another more extreme.

# CHAPTER 28

# Existence

Centralisation may be defined as the referring of everything to some predominating factor. But this definition is merely introductory, as no doubt psychological states could be put forward which superficially met this definition but which I would not accept; and conversely I might very well recognise as centralised something in which there was no overt sign of reference to a central factor.

The operative thing in the psychology of centralisation is that, curiously and at first sight unobviously, it has as a side-effect the facilitation of the perception of existence. (As I have already mentioned, I use 'the perception of existence' to refer to 'the perception of the astonishingness of the fact that existence exists', but I can't say that all the time.) And of course the continuous perception of existence is impossible without a somewhat particular sort of centralisation. The continuous perception of existence, so far as I can see, when referred to at all in the writings of the human race, is usually described as 'impossible'. However, it is not impossible.

I am not, of course, asserting that all forms of centralisation are adequate to produce continuous existential perception, and I am not asserting that all the varieties of centralisation are the same. However all centralised psychology is a different matter from de-centralised or non-centralised psychology.

*

I will demonstrate how centralisation is derived from the perception of the existential uncertainty.

Everything is up to you; you cannot know with certainty that anyone else is there at all (perhaps you are the dreamer and they are in your dream) and even if they are there, there is no reason to suppose that they have any way of judging what is best to be done; nor have you any way of knowing how likely they are to act on their perceptions about this even if they have them, since this is a matter of internal honesty, and only your own mind is available for introspective assessment.

Consequently it is up to you to decide what to do, and to do it.

Clearly there is something to decide *about* (if you accept that the situation is uncertain); you do not know by what criteria to decide to do one thing rather than another, but you are not at liberty to maintain that it is of no importance what you decide. You do not know this; it may be very important or even infinitely important; everything you do may be affecting the fate of the universe or of something more important than the universe. (You cannot appeal to a 'sense of proportion' in face of the incommensurable fact of existence.)

Anyone who thought all this for long enough would become centralised.

*

You can have a kind of social centralisation – i.e. a rather conditioned kind – without seeing existence. E.g. you can be centralised on the idea of your position as a Colonial Governor and relate everything to that. This will produce at least social equivalents of some characteristics of centralised psychology, but it depends on continuing to believe that your status and activities are meaningful. This involves you in a distinct repression of realism at certain points. E.g. if you are risking death, you must not be overcome by the thought that in the presence of annihilation the pottering about of the human race is no concern of yours. On the contrary, you must preserve a strong sense of your position as Her Majesty's representative.

However, even this kind of centralisation is better than nothing. It would make you more likely to have existential flashes in the same way that any intense and directed way of life, with a strong sense of your individual uniqueness, would do so.

The conditions for 'seeing existence' in flashes do not seem to be very rigorous, at least early in life when people have a relatively strong sense of the surprisingness of being themselves.

However, the flashes will not continue unless the person becomes centralised as a result – i.e. adopts as constant criteria the things which feel significant when he is closest to the existential awareness.

The most elementary (but genuine) form is the determination at all times to do what one really wants, and nothing else, because one will die soon. (To do nothing that is beneath one's dignity as protagonist of the universe.) It is fairly obvious that you only *really* want to do important things. To select the most difficult, most purposeful things would be possible as a reaction to death. To select on the basis of ease or pleasure would be unthinkable. (Consider what you would think of doing in the last hour before your execution – social chat?)

Incidentally, the simple reflection that life is very short, if constantly held in mind, would make many kinds of reaction, say irritation, feel vacuous and beneath one's dignity.

# CHAPTER 29

# Royalty

The concept of centralisation is closely related to that of kingship; this is more obvious with the higher forms of centralisation, but even in the elementary forms some relationship may be perceived.

Let us therefore consider analytically why the concept of kingship should have any relationship at all with the ability to perceive the fact of existence. If you do perceive the fact of existence, what you perceive is that you are in a position of the ultimate degree of uncertainty. You have not the slightest idea what everything is existing for, nor what you have got to do with it. You do not know what is important about the situation, nor how important it is. If you are to decide what is to be done about the situation, there is no one to consult but yourself; and you do not know how important your decisions are.

Now human psychology in its ordinary state is not prepared to accept the responsibility for being in this situation; consequently it does not perceive at all that it is in this situation.

And when I talk about 'being in' it, I do not mean verbalising about it, as some existentialists have done. You may of course verbalise about arbitrary decisions, and commitment, and so forth, while remaining entirely within the emotional range of normal psychology.

Now the position of being a king, in its most abstract form, is that you are responsible for deciding about important things, and there is no authority higher than yourself to refer to.

Ordinarily human psychology accepts no responsibility; makes no decisions, has no sense of importance, and believes itself justified in its attitudes by some kind of consensus of social agreement.

(Of course you may say that is too sweeping, and that there are some senses in which people do make decisions, have things they think are important, and so on; but in the sense in which I am meaning these things they certainly do not.)

*

It must be understood that I am using kingship as an entirely psychological concept; unfortunately, I am afraid it will suggest to people associations with political power, and hence of power over other people. However, these associations have nothing to do with the sense in which I am using the concept. I have already said that it is to be understood in the most abstract form, and the only way that power enters into it is in the sense in which someone making decisions of indefinable importance may be said to have power over the situation (whatever it is) in so far as his decisions are able to affect the situation.

*

You may say, if all I am talking about is a psychological position of decision-making in the most abstract sense, why should I prefer the concept of kingship to that of, say, presidenthood. After all, the President of the United States has to make important decisions and there is no higher authority to which he can refer; he is put there by the electorate for just that purpose. However, the trouble with a president or any elected or appointed maker of decisions is that he gets into his position by first obtaining the approval of a number, maybe an inordinately large number, of other people. It is not an intrinsic quality of his own that he is this sort of decision-maker.

On the other hand, the idea of royalty contains an implication of inalienable significance. Few people these days have much to say in favour of the idea of aristocracy; but a hereditary upper class in a society has at least this to recommend it: that there are a number of people who may be a bit freer than the rest of feeling that they have got to prove their worth to other people before they can get on to making up their minds about anything or deciding what is to be done about it. So they are somewhat nearer to the existential decision-making position, and likely to be somewhat better at running things in an effective way in practice.

*

It may be observed that the trend of society at present is very much in favour of a kind of psychology in which one does not feel at all that one is answerable only to oneself, or that however completely one may analyse the factors which enter into a situation, there may always be more which one does not know about. The fashionable way to make a decision is to consult some agent of the collective who will tell you the one or two factors that have been socially agreed upon as what is important in such situations. And you are certainly not permitted to form an assessment of your own of how important something may be to you, existing as you are in the only life you have, or at any rate know about. To conduct your life as if something is of overriding importance to you without having social permission to do so is to arouse a quite unique sort of opprobrium.

I have obtained an interesting sidelight on the process of trying to decide things in a committee by observing the psychological reactions of a number of people attempting to make decisions about investment by discussing them with one another. There is a distinct tendency for the most unreliable kinds of motivation to be much more obtrusive, and to lead to the most vehement and persuasive expressions of opinion, which have a disproportionate influence on the attitudes of the other people concerned. And yet it may transpire in retrospect that several people in the group were *really* wanting to do something different, which would have been much better, but this never achieved effective verbalisation.

In a way this is not surprising, as the most forceful and mechanical parts of people's personalities are probably those which are developed solely in order to interact effectively with other people. So it is not difficult to see that a society which believes in decisions being made by committees will effectively be ensuring that everyone's less socially-conditioned perceptions which might lead them to the right decision will be suppressed. Any one person alone may have some difficulty in distinguishing between those parts of his psychology that are favourable to the making of decisions and those that are not; a number of people in a situation where it is important to say things that will gain the approval of others are virtually certain to make all their decisions with the least reliable parts of all their personalities.

*

The above remarks do not exhaust the significance of the concept of kingship, but merely demonstrate why it is not quite so unreasonable that it should have something to do with being able to live in that emotional range which is compatible with the perception of existence.

# CHAPTER 30

# Courage

I think I should make the point that not all of the attributes of centralisation can be cultivated directly — in fact, in a sense, only centralisation itself can be cultivated directly. I.e. you can try to be single-minded, but you can't try to have, say, courage or initiative.

Courage is anyway very much an external appearance thing. If a person is unconflicted, knows what he wants and wants it strongly, he will obviously be indifferent to things that would put off someone merely acting on social motivation. Hence he will *appear* courageous.

All attempts to produce courage artificially depend on imposing a particularly strong fear of social disapproval or ridicule — even if it be, so to speak, your *own* social disapproval that you try to threaten yourself with. This, therefore, is essentially unrealistic, because it depends on pretending that social approval is more important than your dislike of being reminded that your will can be violated.

And this is what you are reminded of by experiencing any sensation or emotion that you *would not have chosen*.

Thus abject cowardice would be a realistic emotion. However, if genuine and not a social reaction in itself, it would pass into reaction *against* finiteness.

This is a force of at least equal intensity with the will to survive. It is a truism that in peril of death a man may do things he could not ordinarily do — e.g. I remember reading of Nubar Gulbenkian[1] struggling to open the door of an aeroplane which was on fire. The metal door was red-hot (?) — at any rate, very

---

[1] Nubar Gulbenkian was an Armenian oil millionaire, now deceased.

hot – and melting paint fell on his hands. But these facts did not make any impression on him as he struggled, although afterwards he found burns on his hands. (You may argue that this is a dissociated case, and I agree it does not have the lucidity which a centralised reaction to danger would have. But the idea of an overriding intensity is there.)

Ordinary 'social' courage is a conflicted thing. In fact there is something peculiarly horrible in people trying to pretend that they mind what other people think of them in face of pain and death, because no existential solution is possible until they stop pretending this.

True courage is unconflicted; it is one of the paradoxes of centralisation that it isn't even on a continuum with ordinary courage, though it might superficially resemble it.

# CHAPTER 31

# Nostalgia

A graduate who had read English at Oxford once remarked to me that according to Yeats all literature worth its salt deals in the end with only two subjects, Love and Death, and that reading Keats and Wordsworth he (the graduate) was struck by how much of their best poetry is permeated by a consciousness of change.

I suppose poetry would have to be mainly about Love and Death; since it is about such glimmers of intensity as ever visit the benighted mind. Love is commonly the only form in which the human being experiences its desire for the infinite; Death is its most persistent reminder that it is afraid of finiteness. If the human race were a little more advanced, it would want to write poems about infinity and the inconceivable (but perhaps it would not be able to write them) and if it were more advanced still it would have more urgent things to do than write poetry.

Change is almost a subsection of Death perhaps – a reminder that the finite is useless, about which there would be little to say if everyone were not determined to go on making themselves at home in the world. I would find the human race more endearing if it habitually became less stable as it grew older, instead of the reverse.

*

On second thoughts, *are* there any love poems that really come across? I can't think of any, and though at first sight one might blame this on a deficiency of mine, I don't really think this explanation holds water. I do get the point of certain kinds of poetry, even if the emotion conveyed isn't one that I would ever have about those particular things.

There is a distinct class of 'nostalgic' poems which come across to me. Nostalgia is what I call an 'open-ended' emotion. There are other 'open-ended' emotions – e.g. risk-taking – but they are all so disliked by the human race that there are no proper names by which to distinguish them, or talk about them. It is very difficult to describe the emotional attitude of nostalgia or leave-taking without incurring pejorative over-tones; rejection, resignation, disengagement, detachment – all imply something different from what one is trying to say.

I offer you therefore a small anthology of nostalgic verse (and two pieces of prose). Some of it is very familiar, but the point is the common factor. There are a number of forms in which human beings experience a sense of the tragic incompleteness of life; in all of them there is a suggestion, however vague, that the position of man as he is may be pathetic, or proudly tragic, but is basically a position of deprivation.

*

They are not long, the weeping and the laughter,
Love and desire and hate:
I think they have no portion in us after
We pass the gate.


They are not long, the days of wine and roses:
Out of a misty dream
Our path emerges for a while, then closes
Within a dream.

ERNEST DOWSON
(Vitae Summa Brevis)


Ah, Moon of my Delight who know'st no wane,
The Moon of Heav'n is rising once again:
How oft hereafter rising shall she look
Through this same Garden after me — in vain!

*And when Thyself with shining Foot shall pass*
*Among the Guests Star-scatter'd on the Grass,*
*And in thy joyous Errand reach the Spot*
*Where I made one — turn down an empty Glass!*

EDWARD FITZGERALD
(*The Rubá'iyát of Omar Khayyám*)

*Before the beginning of years*
*There came to the making of man*
*Time, with a gift of tears;*
*Grief, with a glass that ran . . .*

*In his heart is a blind desire,*
*In his eyes foreknowledge of death;*
*He weaves, and is clothed with derision;*
*Sows, and he shall not reap;*
*His life is a watch or a vision*
*Between a sleep and a sleep.*

ALGERNON CHARLES SWINBURNE
(*Atalanta in Calydon*)

*We are the music-makers,*
*And we are the dreamers of dreams,*
*Wandering by lone sea-breakers,*
*And sitting by desolate streams; —*
*World-losers and world-forsakers,*
*On whom the pale moon gleams:*
*Yet we are the movers and shakers*
*Of the world for ever, it seems.*

ARTHUR O'SHAUGHNESSY
(*Ode*)

In the following examples the desire becomes more clearly defined; if only we could know there was a purpose, if only we had the apple of the Tree of Knowledge, if only we could get back to the royal city, if only we could take the hidden paths . . .

In the darkness of the night Mr. Hinchcliff had a dream, and saw the valley, and the flaming swords, and the contorted trees, and knew that it really was the Apple of the Tree of Knowledge that he had thrown regardlessly away. And he awoke very unhappy.

In the morning his regret had passed, but afterwards it returned and troubled him; never, however, when he was happy or busily occupied. At last, one moonlight night about eleven, when all Holmwood was quiet, his regrets returned with redoubled force, and therewith an impulse to adventure. He slipped out of the house and over the playground wall, went through the silent town to Station Lane, and climbed into the orchard where he had thrown the fruit. But nothing was to be found of it there among the dewy grass and the faint intangible globes of dandelion down.

H. G. WELLS[1]

*I can give not what men call love,*
*But wilt thou accept not*
*The worship the heart lifts above*
*And the Heavens reject not, —*
*The desire of the moth for the star,*
*Of the night for the morrow,*
*The devotion to something afar*
*From the sphere of our sorrow?*

PERCY BYSSHE SHELLEY
('One Word is too Often Profaned . . .')

*Gondor! Gondor, between the Mountains and the Sea!*
*West Wind blew there; the light upon the Silver Tree*
*Fell like bright rain in gardens of the Kings of old.*
*O proud walls! White towers! O winged crown and throne of gold!*
*O Gondor, Gondor! Shall Men behold the Silver Tree,*
*Or West Wind blow again between the Mountains and the Sea?*

J. R. R. TOLKIEN
(The Lord of the Rings, Vol. II, p. 25)

[1] H. G. Wells, *The Apple*, included in *Complete Short Stories*, Ernest Benn Ltd., London, 1927, p. 402.

*Still round the corner there may wait*
*A new road or a secret gate;*
*And though I oft have passed them by,*
*A day will come at last when I*
*Shall take the hidden paths that run*
*West of the Moon, East of the Sun.*

J. R. R. TOLKIEN
*(The Lord of the Rings,* Vol. III, p. 308)

The following expression of nostalgia may, it is true, be read as an expression of arrival rather than of desire; but in fact the thing which is arrived at remains undefined, and I think the chief effect of the passage on the reader is to arouse a sense of something indefinable which might be indefinably and immeasurably to be desired.

### Death of Sparkenbroke

Opening the gate of the Mound, he went in, not in the hope of renewal before the world that had brought him often to this place, nor in the desire of visions of manifest powers, nor in the tumult of spirit which cries: Speak, yet cannot hear for its own outcrying, nor in the ambition of knowledge, nor in the pride of angels, but in certitude of that divine presence which, formerly apprehended as but the mediate essence of created things, was now immediate and everlasting, an absolute singleness exempt from the division of forms.

In this he stood, at first in wonder, for it was external to him, and he as yet armoured in the body, himself, alone; but, by the last pang of the body, it came into him, as the sun into a candle, so ravishing and including him that wonder laid down its arms and imagination its images.

CHARLES MORGAN[1]

The final example is a poem I wrote myself when I was in my first year at college.

[1] Charles Morgan, *Sparkenbroke*, Macmillan & Co. Ltd., London, 1936, pp. 549–50.

*Oh my intangible unnamed loss;*
*I will weep useless tears like a lost child;*
*I am unknown to myself and unfulfilled;*
*Oh but I hate and hate you,*
*All you who were responsible for this;*
*And I walk with no faith and little joy*
*Seeking my homelessness.*

Some people have found the word 'homelessness' in the last line surprising, as if they thought homelessness was not a thing to go in search of, and they would have expected some word like 'home' instead.

Actually this word reflects the fact that, at the time, I had been reduced as nearly as possible to perceiving the world on the normal terms, but, I must believe, still not as most people see it, because to me it was barren. Nevertheless I saw it as a source of security; a security I did not want; a system which seemed closed and complete, fitting together in only one possible way. I might remember, abstractly, that there had been a time when I had perceived that uncertainty was the last word in every philosophical argument, but the world as everyone saw it was all that could be perceived in every direction. Now I have forgotten again how to see the world as a source of security, so it is difficult for me to represent to myself how oppressive this was.

\*

What has nostalgia to do with existence? — Well, this. It is open-ended. Most common emotions are not. All sensible, mature emotions are not. (Johnson, for example, is never open-ended.) Perceptions about existence are open-ended *par excellence*; they admit of no security whatever and only an unconditional realism will tolerate them. Evidently people whose common emotions are not open-ended may be expected to have few emotions about the inconceivable, or none.

\*

I cannot define open-endedness, except ostensively. It is a quality of emotion, and emotions are not always about what they appear to be. All the nostalgic pieces I quoted are approximately equivalent in having a quality of letting go; saying: 'All *that* I leave – even if only while I stand aside to write this – it is nothing to do with me any more.' Some of them say also, and others do not, 'There is something else, quite other than all this, that I cannot give any name to, and this only I desire.' I would say that this is implicit in the quality of the emotion, even if it is not stated.

Johnson, in *Rasselas*,[1] writes on old age. This might be nostalgic (in the present sense of the word) but is not. His old man says, 'Nothing in the world is any use to me now,' but not, 'I see it all and take my leave of it.' There is no shifting of perspective so that life is seen from the outside. It is seen from the same place, but it looks emptier. His old man says, 'I have projected many things, and I have failed to bring them about,' and not, 'I see that all I have projected was too little; now I will desire a greater thing.' There is no change in valuation at all; the only difference is that the old man is no longer in a position to start new projects or complete old ones.

On a verbal level you might claim that the old man expresses everything necessary for open-ended nostalgia; he even says 'Now I have no hope in this life and must hope for something beyond it,' – but if you pay attention you see that he is not wanting anything *different* at all – he merely hopes 'to possess in a better state that happiness which here I could not find, and that virtue which here I have not attained.' (This last is an accurate quotation; the rest are free paraphrases.)

And that brings us to the question of survival, illustrating as it does the fact that when people believe in, or wish for, survival, they are usually thinking of a continuation of their life much as it is. (It is rather like a fly desiring to spend eternity on a flypaper, confident that given only time enough it can find how not to be incommoded by the stickiness.)

I had better state my own position, since it is not common. I do not see that temporal extension of this kind of consciousness would provide any solution at all; but admittedly this attitude

[1] Samuel Johnson, *History of Rasselas, Prince of Abyssinia*, Oxford University Press, 1887.

depends on the fact that I regard a position of ignorance as something requiring a solution. If you value consciousness as providing opportunities for various kinds of pleasure rather than as a means to knowledge, I suppose continuation of it in its present state might seem desirable.

On account of the uncertainty inherent in all knowledge, I do not see how the possibility of my consciousness being annihilated could ever be eliminated even if 'survival' could be shown to be a possibility.

In fact it is logically impossible for 'survival' to be demonstrated, in the same way that it is logically impossible for the existence of *consciousness* behind anyone else's behaviour to be demonstrated. For example: if a medium produces an apparently precise reproduction of the modes of expression and resources of information possessed by a deceased person, this may still be a dramatisation by the medium based on telepathically acquired information about the deceased. A number of people have found reproductions of this kind so convincing that they have said 'It was indistinguishable from talking to X in person.' Behaviourists who think it irrelevant to enquire whether *consciousness* is *present* should, to be consistent, be the first to believe in survival on this evidence. For in other contexts they will repeat indefatigably: 'What we *mean* by someone *being* X is that we recognise his mannerisms and get the kind of responses we associate with X; this is what we *mean* by personal identity.'

*

*Postscript*. As well as saying, Our happiness is here or not at all, or words to that effect, Wordsworth also once wrote:

> *Whether we be young or old,*
> *Our destiny, our being's heart and home,*
> *Is with infinitude, and only there;*
> *With hope it is, hope that can never die,*
> *Effort, and expectation, and desire,*
> *And something evermore about to be.*
>
> The Prelude, VI, 603

Not that I think that is open-ended; but it is, at least ostensibly, about open-endedness.

CHAPTER 32

# Open-endedness

*Existential Music*

1. Wagner: Opening of Act III of *Die Walküre* ('The Ride of the Valkyries').
2. Schubert: *Impromptu* in A flat major, Opus 142, No. 2.
3. Coates: March: 'The Dam Busters'.
4. Tchaikovsky: Piano Concerto No. 1: first 24 bars.
5. Wagner: Close of *Das Rheingold* ('Entry of the Gods into Valhalla').

(This list not only contains all the existential music known to me, if the rest of the Schubert Impromptus are added to it; but, played in this order, it may be taken as constituting a psychological sequence.)

\*

I do not know if I am making much progress in elucidating the application of the existential criterion to psychology. Perhaps the selection of music which I quoted may serve as an illustration. I do not claim that any of the composers were necessarily seeing existence at the time, but at least they might have been.

Nearly all music, on the contrary, contains emotional components which make it quite certain that the composer was debarred from the perception of existence at the time, and probably all the time.

The cosiness, gregariousness, and *jollity* which occur in Handel's 'Messiah', for example, rule him right out of court. This element of jollity, frolic, irresponsibility, degraded enjoyment – whatever one is to call it – occurs also in Beethoven and in many other places.

We might agree to use the word 'jollity' for this stiflingly enclosed anti-existential component, and contrast it with what we might agree to call 'elation'. (We might then say that Schubert perhaps touched upon the elation of despair.)

The one, you will perceive, is open-ended; the other is not.

I suppose that I have not yet demonstrated at all exhaustively why centralisation of the personality should be favourable to existential perceptions – but 'jollity' provides at any rate one example of an emotion which is perceptibly decentralised and also perceptibly not open-ended. It is illuminating that the language has no single word to denote the element of 'enjoyment of irresponsibility, acceptance of a degraded position' which enters into most known kinds of gaiety or exuberance.

'To accept one's limitations' is an unrealistic emotional action, because it ignores the presence of the total uncertainty. It is also incompatible with open-endedness, by reason of the limitation of mental horizons which follows from it. It follows that any form of rejoicing which includes acceptance of a limited position in the scheme of things is certain to be anti-existential.

It always amuses me to rewrite theology. The unforgivable sin has been said to be blasphemy against the Holy Spirit, and this has been interpreted to refer to 'despair'. It is plain that the human race is in a state of complete despair, because they all accept their limitations and live, without hope, in an attitude of profound disrespect towards the incalculable possibilities implied by the total uncertainty.

It should also be noticed that the existential analogues of 'acceptance' and 'resignation' are aggressive emotions. The Schubert partially, though not perfectly, illustrates this.

It may also be noticed in passing how much of mutually accepted and enforced degradation enters into most forms of conviviality, mutuality, and 'humour'. The existential analogue of humour is virtually unrecognisable; it arises out of the fact that inconceivable risks are to be taken at every moment. The humour to which this gives rise is a more extreme form of the elation of despair.

# CHAPTER 33

# Male *versus* Female Psychology

It is interesting to apply the existential criterion to the various characteristics which compose the female image. (I use the expression 'female image' to denote that psychological syndrome supposedly possessed by female humans.)

In the first place females are supposed to be *dependent* rather than independent. It is clear that dependence is not an imaginable attitude for anyone who is aware of the total uncertainty, since it is plain that no one else can be expected to have any superior insight into the problem. But even if it is not taken on so abstract a level, it is clear that no one could be certain when they might not find themselves confronted by a situation in which no human assistance was accessible. In such a situation, which might occur at any moment (as a result of a tidal wave following the fall of a meteor into the Pacific Ocean, for example) anyone might be obliged to act on their own resources. No one with any awareness, on even a physical level, of the risks incurred in the human situation on this planet could find the cultivation of 'dependent' habits of reaction to situations other than blood-curdling.

Further, women are supposed to be *subjective* rather than objective. It is clear that objectivity is far more favourable for the appreciation of facts, and on a criterion of realism is evidently to be preferred.

Further, women are supposed to be *unambitious* and particularly *interested in human relationships*. It will be observed that this conjunction of qualities is precisely what is to be expected from the account already given of the way in which the desire for transcendence becomes deflected into compensatory interactions with other people.

Finally, women are supposed to be particularly *unadventurous*, security-seeking, and comfort-loving. It is clear that no such attitudes are compatible with a perception of the total insecurity of the position.

The existential criterion does not, of course, enable us to determine whether the psychological characteristics are (a) fictitious, (b) actually present but the result of social conditioning, or (c) actually present and the result of physiological influences. All the existential criterion enables us to say is that these psychological characteristics, whenever and from whatever cause they are present, will not be favourable to the perception of existence and therefore to centralised psychology in general.

*

Once, in a harassed state, when I was trying to cope with a situation which involved myself, Gurdjieff, and three women, I asked him: 'Why do you let them stay here when they say such things about you, when they oppose you in every way?'

He said: 'You not understand; they do not say what they really feel. Men are logical, women not logical. You make mistake because you expect a woman to react as a man would react. Men are men. Women are women.'[1]

It is clear from this book that Gurdjieff thinks in terms of two distinct ideal personality structures for men and women respectively. Although it is claimed that stable marriages resulted from his treatment, it is not on record that any of the women in question reached a very vivid awareness of the existential astonishment.

In fact, there is only one kind of centralised personality structure and it is most likely to be reflected in the ideal self-image held by upper-class males in a consciously dominant society. This follows from the fact that it is based upon existential 'responsibility' and is not likely to be reflected in the ethos of any subdominant or irresponsible section of society. (It does not follow that *any* section of society is likely to hold very

[1] C. S. Nott, *Teachings of Gurdjieff*, Routledge & Kegan Paul, London, 1961, p. 113.

157

enlightened views about how to educate people to be centralised; it is the ideal only that is of interest, and that is, even at its
best, distorted by the translation into social terms.)

*

If you make a list of the attributes supposed to be typically
masculine and those supposed to be typically feminine, you find
you have a description of centralisation on the one hand and of
decentralisation on the other. E.g. independence, initiative,
consistency, objectivity, courage, *versus* dependence, submis-
siveness, inconsistency, subjectivity, timidity.

I do not mean to exclude, say, sensitivity and generosity from
the male image; but such things are in any case the prerogatives
of assurance. The conciliations of feebleness are a different
matter altogether.

Now Freud, although describing how women progress from
the desire to be given a penis by their father to the compensatory
desire to be given a baby by their husband, sees nothing
fundamentally wrong in this state of affairs. One might suppose
that on realising their original wish in life was to be freed from
the female image, the appropriate thing to do might be to
abandon it. It is true that if all women thought of themselves as
men the birth-rate of the human race would drop noticeably.
But I do not claim to be giving a prescription for preserving the
*status quo*.

Nietzsche, again, although his observations were not wholly
inaccurate, did not break with the prejudice that it must, in
some way, be appropriate for half the human race to be like
this.

Incidentally, *à propos* Nietzsche's views on women: it is true
(after a fashion) that men are children at heart and women are
not. Women abandoned themselves to society younger.

*

To revert to the existential criterion: how can you 'want
security' in the presence of the existential uncertainty? Want to
drift round aimlessly in the only existence you have? Want to be

158

dependent on another fragile mortal? Want to spend your attention on 'human problems' when you do not know what is the point of the little animals called humans being there at all?

However, the situation is simple if the supposed female personality is regarded as a myth. It is in fact a compensation, and a fragile one, and any stability it seems to have is the stability of the human evasion itself.

This explains also the alleged emotional instability of women; they are kept in a permanently decentralised state. It is a natural outcome of this that their hatred and resentment should at times break through, though it is unlikely that they will take the responsibility for having these feelings; hence the appearance of irrationality.

For example, the kind of 'irrationality' described in connection with Gurdjieff's women is sufficiently explained by their repressed resentment at being kept in a decentralised position.

*

Centralised psychology is not compatible with trying to prove things to other people, which is one reason why it is not very compatible with any standard female psychological image. The female is supposed to be more orientated towards pleasing other people, and actually is often very concerned that everyone else should be devoting enough attention to worrying about what other people are thinking.

This is almost synonymous with the fact that centralised psychology depends on being responsible for what you are really in control of, and not trying to be responsible for what you are not. The relationship arises from the fact that the pressure to prove things to other people almost always results in a pressure to try to be responsible for things you cannot be.

Actually people commonly apply centralised psychology inversely; that is, they are irresponsible about what they could really control and make use of, and allow themselves to feel responsible for things that are not under their control.

The things that are not under people's control usually consist of parts of their own psychology which they think they should be able to make to work in certain ways, and the attitudes of other people, which, they allow themselves to be persuaded, they should be able to influence in certain ways by merit or persuasion.

# CHAPTER 34

# Religion

All basic religious ideas can be expressed in two forms: one personal and the other existential. In the first case the result is obnoxious, and in the second dangerous to common sense. The human race prefers to consider only the obnoxious versions, whether accepting or rejecting them. To do it justice, it must be admitted that it does not *say* that the existential versions are dangerous. For the most part it ignores them, and if they are forced upon its attention it calls them cold, negative, intellectual, metaphysical – and so on.

So you *can* say (but no one does): within the inconceivable there is scope for many orders of significance, each totally overriding those beneath it; and in particular, the reason for which existence exists must, in at least a certain sense, be more important than any purpose that can be formulated in terms of that which exists.

But in fact the nearest approximation to such an idea is stated – by someone like C. S. Lewis – in some such form as: God has super-fatherly rights to obedience from his creatures because he created them for his pleasure, not their own. This repellent situation leaves you a choice between emotional attitudes called 'rebellion' and 'submission'. If you accept this formulation of the situation, there is virtually no scope for an existential reaction – i.e. for any reaction which releases your psychology from unrealism.

Since I have defined two characteristics of existential psychology – i.e. centralisation and open-endedness – you may see that it would be very hard to react to this situation in a way that had either of these qualities. Perhaps the best one could do would be a Shelleian attitude of anti-authoritarianism, which consists of a determination to be open-ended in spite of every-thing.

Milton's Satan is half centralised and half reactive; insofar as he is centralised he is noticeably heroic. But Milton confuses two things, the existential and the personal. When Satan is heroic he might be seen as reacting to impersonal adversity in the spirit of Henley's *Invictus*. When he is reactive he is just trying to do something that God won't like – not because he, Satan, has any intrinsic reason for doing it. 'Evil, be thou my good' means '*I* shall regard as good anything *you* think is evil' – and this is in antithesis to the centralised position: 'I shall regard as good what *I* regard as good, whatever *you* may think.'

('*Reactive*' in my terminology means 'directed towards producing an effect on other people in reaction to or against something they have previously done to you'.)

# CHAPTER 35

# Gnostic Christianity

When I attempt to read the literary productions of the human race I usually feel as if I have stumbled into the fantasy world of a psychotic. In Dante's fantasy world, for example, people are tortured. ('The world's greatest poem.') In Cervantes's, idealism is pilloried. And so on.

It is therefore worthy of note as a phenomenon that I find a streak of something not wholly disagreeable in Gnostic Christianity. My attempts to inform myself about the historical situation have led me only to the conclusion that, since the human race has never been interested in facts, it is natural for their documents to be vague. Any precision they seem to possess is to be viewed with the deepest misgiving.

I conclude, however, that there was almost certainly a person (or semi-person) alive somewhere in the Eastern Mediterranean region within a few centuries each way of the presumed life of Christ.

I should feel less confident of this if I had to base it on the synoptic Gospels alone. It is true that even they contain a handful of sayings which might have been said by a non-sane person, and which it is difficult to imagine anyone else inventing or wishing to pass on, but these are to be found among so much wadding in the way of detailed itineraries of perambulations round the lake and moral instruction of an uninteresting kind that one might wonder if one were not straining the whole thing too much in seeking out and mentally juxtaposing the interesting elements.

The existence of the *Gospel of Thomas*, however, goes far to confirm one's impression that somebody, somehow, had got to know something about psychology. It is, from my point of view, a far more interesting document than the synoptic Gospels. It leaves out everything one finds difficult in the synoptics, and includes a number of directly existential sayings which find no parallels in them.

Now you may, of course, say that Christ really meant his teaching to be like the synoptics, only more so. That all the elements in the synoptics which I find interesting were Gnostic pollutions, and that the compiler of *Thomas* is responsible for the existential bits.

In that case it may be that the existential person in question was the anonymous author of *Thomas*. But I am not arguing about questions of identity.

The sayings in *Thomas* which find no parallels in the synoptics greatly strengthen the existential case.

E.g.

*References to existential perception:*

Jesus said:
>Know what is before your face,
>and what is hidden from you will be revealed to you;
>for there is nothing hidden which will not be manifest.[1]

His disciples said to him:
>On what day does the kingdom come?
(Jesus said:)
>It does not come when it is expected.
>They will not say, Lo, here! or Lo, there!
>But the kingdom of the Father
>is spread out upon the earth, and men do not see it.[2]

*References to centralisation:*

Jesus said:
>Let him who seeks not cease in his seeking until he finds;
>and when he finds, he will be troubled,
>and if he is troubled, he will marvel,
>˄nd will be a king over the All.[3]

˄t *Sayings of Jesus*, edited by Robert M. Grant and David N.
˄s Fontana Books, London, 1960, p. 118, Saying no. 4.
˄. 111.          [3] Ibid., p. 114, no. 1.

164

Jesus said:
   May he who has become rich become a king,
   and may he who has power deny (the world).[1]


*References to the prevalence of non-existential psychology (somewhat over-optimistic, however):*

Jesus said:
   I will choose you,
   one from a thousand and two from ten thousand,
   and they will stand because they are a single one.[2]

Jesus said:
   I stood in the midst of the world
      and I appeared to them in the flesh;
   I found all of them drunken;
      I found none among them thirsty,
   And my soul was pained for the children of men,
      for they are blind in their hearts,
      and they do not see
      that they came empty into the world
      seeking also to leave the world empty.
   But now they are drunken.
      When they throw off their wine,
      then they will repent.[3]


*An expression of disrespect for the non-existential past:*

His disciples said to him:
   Twenty-four prophets spoke in Israel,
   and all of them spoke concerning you.
He said to them:
   You have abandoned the one who lives before your eyes,
   and you have spoken concerning the dead.[4]


*A psychological perception (true, but not common knowledge):*

Simon Peter said to them:
   Let Mariham go away from us.
   For women are not worthy of life.

[1] Ibid., p. 169, no. 81.
[2] Ibid., p. 137, no. 24.
[3] Ibid., p. 140, no. 29.
[4] Ibid., p. 153, no. 53.

Jesus said:
> Lo, I will draw her
> so that I will make her a man
> so that she too may become a living spirit
> which is like you men;
> for every woman who makes herself a man
> will enter into the kingdom of heaven.[1]

Now it is clear that, whatever the author's sources may have been, this collection of sayings has been determined by reference to more or less existential criteria (or at any rate they do not include anything which is unambiguously rebarbative by reference to such criteria, though many of the sayings are unclear). It is also clear that the synoptic gospels have not been selected by reference to such criteria, although they contain a number of sayings (small in proportion to their total length) which pass them.

The Gnostic church, which did not survive, and the church which is now regarded as orthodox were thus operating on different psychological criteria. This makes considerations of dating much less relevant. The earliest document in the field can only claim primacy in a situation in which it is believed that no distorting factors were at work other than unavoidable errors of transmission.

It is claimed that the synoptic gospels antedate the Gospel of Thomas. But in assessing this fact one must bear in mind that the Gnostics were persecuted by the orthodox Church, and every effort was made to destroy Gnostic writings. A population of documents, subject to copying, resembles a population of animals, reproducing. If you take two populations of animals and decimate one annually while protecting the other, there will, after a certain time has elapsed, be a distinct probability that the oldest survivors will form part of the protected population.

But even this reflection is not much to the point. Nothing can relieve you of the necessity of *deciding* which set of

[1] Ibid., p. 185, no. 112.

psychological criteria the nominal originator of these variant forms would have approved of.

If you decide that he would have approved of the synoptic set, I think to be consistent you must eliminate from the synoptics their existential elements (which would be no great loss, since they are studiously ignored in any case). But I at any rate find it implausible that someone accidentally uttered a few sayings which might have been said by an existential person, and after his death a rather wild editor added some more which accidentally rounded out a fairly complete, if sketchy, set of existential opinions.

It is no explanation to say that the Gnostics as a movement were more or less existential.[1] No group will be found holding existential opinions unless they have been originated by an existential individual; and the tendency will never be for the opinions of the group to become more existential with the passage of time.

I do not mean to suggest that any explanation of the facts is without difficulties. But the very fact that I can find no completely convincing way of accounting for the 'historical' evidence suggests that some of it is actively misleading. And this is really only to be expected if, in fact, there was a non-sane individual somewhere around the origins of Christianity or of Gnosticism. The tendency to present such a person as something quite different from what he actually was can scarcely be overestimated.

[1] When I use the adjective 'existential' to refer to a person, group, psychology, etc., I mean it to refer to a psychological disposition which might favour relatively frequent perceptions about existence.

CHAPTER 36

# The Origins of Christianity

In the last chapter I referred to the difficulties which arise from a consideration of the historical evidence connected with the origins of Christianity. I shall illustrate the difficulties with reference to the Dead Sea Scrolls.

It appears that there was a religious sect at Qumran for a matter of about two centuries, starting about one century before the putative life of Christ.

Let us put the psychological evidence first. I find the utterances of this sect unattractive. They had no noticeable interest in reality; they believed very hard in Society; they had a lot of very strict and pointless rules and penalised one another very severely for any breach of them. Their documents abound in such expressions as: righteous . . . seduce . . . rectitude . . . commandment . . . humble . . . rebel . . . mercy . . . iniquity . . . etc., etc.

In fact, the familiar stuff of religions about Society.

This sect had a 'Teacher of Righteousness', and there is some reason to suppose that this person may have been crucified, with a number of followers. Attempts to identify Jesus with this Teacher do not convince me, because I cannot imagine even the Christ of the synoptics associating with these people.

('Every man will be placed according to his rank. First the priests will sit down, second the elders . . . The man who is asked to do so shall speak in his turn. And in a session of the Many, let no man say anything displeasing to the majority or which is not by the direction of the Overseer . . .')[1]

This is not to say that the life history of the Teacher of

[1] John Allegro, *The Dead Sea Scrolls*, Penguin Books, Middlesex, 1956, p. 112.

168

Righteousness may not have become amalgamated with the life history of Christ.

Incidentally, my confidence in the historicity of the name Jesus is not increased by the fact that its Hebrew form 'Joshua' embodies the idea of 'save'.

The Qumran sect certainly had ideas about a Messiah, about a coming battle between the powers of Light and Darkness, and about a millennium. It may be thought that such ideas would be natural to a subject people; and there is nothing about the expression of the ideas that makes their interpretation on a merely political level implausible – or, at any rate, as *motivated* on a political or psychiatric level.

What does the theology of the early Church (and post-Pauline theology is the earliest we know) add to the ideas of sects such as this? All the contorted stuff about sin and atonement and judgement and mercy would have been quite comprehensible to these people. The idea of being made perfect by the grace of God although you are sinful really and no merit of your own is involved was understood by them with crystal clarity. They had solemn ritual meals continually.

There is actually very little, if anything, in Christian theology which is not within the emotional range of these people. It is only necessary to incorporate the idea of a blood-sacrifice – not an astonishingly unheard-of idea.

What, at any rate, does positively emerge is that we do not have to look further for the origins of some of the *un*interesting elements in the synoptics. Thus, the prescriptions of Matthew 18: 15–17 (about how you first criticise your brother, and then you criticise him before witnesses and then you criticise him before more witnesses – showing a typically sane faith in the agreement of a multiplicity of persons) are closely paralleled in the *Manual of Discipline* of the Qumran sect.

The almost Jungian dishonesty of the Gospel of St. John is also shown to have unmistakeable affinities with the writings of this sect. 'No longer can John be regarded as the most Hellenistic of the Evangelists; his 'gnosticism' and the whole framework of his thought is seen now to spring directly from a Jewish sectarianism rooted in Palestinian soil . . .'[1] That shows, incidentally, how misleading it is to try to trace the affinities of ideas without considering their psychological characteristics. I should never have dreamed of associating the Gospel of John with Gnosticism.

This latter consideration reminds me how very suspect are the judgements of scholars in this field. For example, they postulate a pre-Christian Gnosticism. As far as I know, they have no reason for this except that they cannot see where the ideas originated. (Naturally, they disregard the possibility of an individual actually thinking.)

It also emerges that there was probably a very early kind of uninteresting Christianity. ('. . . one section of the very early *Didache* or 'Teaching of the Twelve Apostles', dealing with 'The Two Ways', could almost be a literal translation of . . . part of The Qumran *Manual of Discipline*.')[2]

If the Qumran Teacher of Righteousness is to be identified with the Christ of the synoptics, someone else said the existential bits and became the Christ of the Gnostics. But what were either of them doing preaching to masses around lakes? The Qumran Teacher of Righteousness would have been busy keeping the rules in his monastery. The Christ of the Gnostics would not expect the masses to understand. (The Gospel of Thomas, incidentally, spares us this difficulty. It gives no indication of spatial location whatever.)

There is, I allow, a partial loophole. The peregrinations of the Gospels cannot cover a very long period of time, and may cover a very short one. (Scholarly estimates range between one and three years.) The Christ of the Gnostics might occasionally have gone hunting recruits, although he would not have expected to find many. No doubt he would have preferred to do it by disseminating written material, but in those days that would not have been possible. Even then, though, I find the procedure of preaching to crowds dubious. The people he wanted might not come. The people he didn't want might come all too often. The door to

[1] Ibid., p. 143.
[2] Ibid., p. 142.

door approach would be more reliable and scarcely more exhausting.

*

Quotation by Frazer from Dio Chrystostom's description of the Sacaea:

> They take one of the prisoners condemned to death, and seat him upon the king's throne, and give him the king's raiment, and let him lord it . . . But afterwards they strip and scourge and crucify him.[1]

Frazer produces many parallels to the sacrificial theme of orthodox Christianity. This leads him to suppose that Christ — i.e. the person the Gospels purport to be about — actually became involved in a traditional ritual murder. But my confidence in the historical status of the Gospels is not so great as to necessitate this hypothesis; I require some evidence that a narrative is more than fictional before 'explaining' it as fact. What Frazer certainly does is to suggest sources from which many of the narrative details of the Gospels might have been derived. We may say: so many of the details are in conformity with the requirements of certain techniques of ritual murder that it would be odd if they had happened spontaneously without actually forming part of such a ritual. But this does not prove that such a ritual murder actually happened to the person that the Gospels are ostensibly about, nor, indeed, that the person the Gospels are ostensibly about corresponds to any person or persons who actually lived.

More generally, Frazer calls attention to the tendency of the human race to set up gods and priest-kings for the sole purpose of killing them off after a short time for the welfare of the community. If this tendency exists — and it may well do — I do not find it necessary to invoke erroneous inferences by feeble-minded Stone Age men about the fertilising properties of royal corpses to explain it. It is sufficient to suppose that the human race has always disliked centralised psychology and has wished,

---

[1] Sir James Frazer, *The Golden Bough* (3rd edition), Macmillan, London, 1913, Vol. IX, p. 414. The Sacaea was a Babylonian festival.

at fairly frequent intervals, symbolically to destroy it. No doubt this procedure is very nourishing to normal psychology; hence the assumption that great benefits to the community would accrue, symbolised and to a variable extent identified with flourishing harvests.

# CHAPTER 37

# Christ

I have been looking back at some earlier chapters and I see that I quoted Grenfell and Henley. Well, they're pretty awful really, of course. To see anything in Grenfell in particular you have to forget completely the situation he is actually writing about, and make copious allowances for unrealistic assumptions.

And, of course, you may have something if you say that it is a fairly common kind of reaction to danger. It is obviously dissociated, for one thing. Dissociation eliminates awareness of some of the facts; existential awareness includes more facts, which may greatly modify the appearance of the normal ones. A state of genuine existential awareness could never be described as 'made blind'.

Dissociated reactions to danger, elated or not, are far more common than realistically elated ones. In general, human psychology is arranged so that it will accept fragments of existential experience only when it is in a dissociated state. This ensures that (a) the existential experience will be distorted, and (b) that it will have no effect on the personality structure of the experient.

But then I do not claim that any idea of existential psychology can be gained from the accumulated literature of the human race; I quote such things as Grenfell only because they're the nearest there is in certain respects.

And then again, when I talk as if there might have been an existential person around the time of Christ, I can't guarantee that whoever it was wasn't dissociated or dishonest. I should like to say that certain perceptions guaranteed unalloyed existentialness in the percipient. In fact I can only say that the dishonesty of which human psychology is capable continually surprises me.

I do not think it is possible to perceive the unknowability of existence and simultaneously to be dishonest. But it is certainly possible to be so subsequently, and it is also possible to be dishonest about whether you were perceiving the unknowability of existence at all. So I cannot take the presence of recognisably existential references as any particular guarantee of anything; Hume, after all, makes recognisable references to existence.

But I sometimes find it convenient to argue as if there was an existential person around the time of Christ. This is because it can be argued about. A completely existential person is an assessable proposition; so are the distortions which other people might create around such a person. But the psychology of a dishonest person with a certain number of existential perceptions is a matter for astonishment and wild surmise.

For example, if one makes the assumption of existentialness, one arrives at a certain estimate of the age of Christ (or whoever it was). This is arrived at as follows:—

There are two weaknesses in the Gospel of Thomas (and Gnosticism generally). They both come in areas where human psychology is known to have great resistances.

For one thing there is little concept of urgency, or of the importance of any overriding purpose. But there is no need to trace this back to the existential originator. The Gospel of Thomas has a certain literary air; the author is having time to be aesthetic. What he presents is unconditionality; but not urgency.

Oddly enough, there is more feeling of something like urgency or purposiveness in the synoptic Gospels. At least, if you take the urgent statements together you get a feeling of a certain impatience; but if you take them separately they are often a little off — too crude, too ordinary, too hot, too personal. I mean, it is pointless calling people a generation of vipers. But perhaps that bit was the Teacher of Righteousness.

However; I am prepared to make a lot of allowance for

174

distortion in transmission. A detached urgency would be easily misrepresented.

A more serious weakness is the leniency with which the psychology of humans at large is described. You cannot ascribe the state of man to drowsiness, stupor, ignorance, or any other accidental effect. The state of man is intensely motivated. If the existential originator had had an altogether more forceful explanation of the motivation of normal psychology, although the author of Thomas might have wished to suppress it, would he have had the subtlety to replace it by a softer and less harmful version? It seems more likely that he would have suppressed it altogether – particularly as the softer version is such as an existential person might hold, but only if he had not had long in which to observe human psychology.

I think the probability is that this weakness must be laid at the door of the originator; in which case two explanations are possible. Either he was dishonest, or he was very young – more probably under twenty than over it.

I am aware that no tradition supports this view. But sane people might not want the central authority in their paternalistic religion to appear too young . . .

I do not feel that attempts to date the life of Christ by reference to historical events referred to in the Gospels add much to the argument. I don't have that much respect for the Gospels as historical texts.

You have only to consider how small a portion of the alleged life of Christ is on record at all to ask why the rest was suppressed. If there was an actual person, someone, at some point, must have known much more than we do about his movements throughout his life. But no mention of these movements remain in the surviving records. It is difficult not to infer from this that, for some reason, the early Church did not wish anything about the rest of his life to be known. It would be interesting to know whether the Gnostic church had a different set of biographical data . . . (But this we shall never know unless the human race accidentally finds some documents, is thwarted by the fates in its attempts to lose them again, and can find no reason to postpone publishing them for more than a decade or so.)

If there was an existential person, it is not plausible that he could live for thirty years or so without acting in a purposeful way. People have existential impulses, if at all, when they are very young. If they betray such impulses they do not recover; they proceed to betray them more. If they do not betray them they remain noticeably existential, and do not waste time on actions which are irrelevant to their purpose. So no explanation in terms of 'His Mission only started when he was thirty' will wash.

The area of suppression is enormous if we are dealing with someone who died in his thirties, forties or fifties, as various scholars surmise. But the total silence would find a partial explanation if in fact whoever it was actually died at about twenty. There might still be things to suppress, but in terms of sheer physical activity there could not be so much.

Even if he died at twenty, though, I think one should not underestimate the quantity of getting around he might have had time for. Existential people are almost certain to seem extremely precocious when judged by the degree of arrested development which is the general state of young persons in a non-existential world. (I don't mean to imply that the development of non-existential people stops being arrested when they grow up.)

*

This reminds me of the 'simple, down-to-earth, man-of-the-people' fallacy.

Christ is supposed to have been uneducated. Oh well; come to that I am uneducated. At any rate, no one educated me. Why do they never even entertain the possibility that someone might have had an I.Q.?

There is such a thing as autonomous mental activity; it is obviously quite distinct from the acquisition of the fashionable associations of ideas. I have always been unable to acquire fashionable associations of ideas, and I should be quite unable to function successfully as a modern mathematician, physicist, philosopher, or psychologist. That is not to say that I despise my abilities as a mathematician, physicist, philosopher, or psychologist. But the unfashionability of my ways of thought should make it clear that they cannot be regarded as *learnt*.

But if someone had a high I.Q. and saw through society sufficiently to take the most direct routes towards anything he wanted to know about, I see no difficulty in supposing that he could know all he wanted to know about any philosophical ideas current in his time, and that he could read, write and speak any languages which he regarded as sufficiently useful.

I remain unconvinced by arguments that he knew only Aramaic because most people of that place and time knew only Aramaic; that he could not read or write because we have no record of his having been subjected to a formal education; that he never travelled because we have no records of the travels, and so on.

Incidentally, if he *could* read and write, why did nothing written by him survive?

# CHAPTER 38

# Taking Thought for the Morrow

My interpretations of the New Testament are all based on the simple process of thinking what I might have meant myself if I had said such a thing; if I can think of nothing I think that remotely corresponds I take it that it doesn't derive from anyone existential.

So the most interesting sense I can give to 'Take no thought for the morrow' is that 'morrow' actually refers to 'the state of affairs that will prevail when you are continuously aware of the total uncertainty', or, even, the ultimate in hypotheticalness, 'the state of affairs that would prevail if everybody were continuously aware of the total uncertainty'.

People do, rather frequently and persistently in my experience, assert that they cannot possibly alter their attitude to the here and now, or the structure of society, in any particular, without bringing about some consequence which (in the light of their present outlook) would be disastrous. For example, people are frequently under the impression that if they stopped believing very hard in human life as it is at present lived, which involves excluding from their minds an awareness of how much in their attitude to it is in fact an arbitrary choice on their own part, they would be unable to manage their affairs efficiently, earn money, etc. Another very common line of argument is that to adopt a critical attitude towards social agreement as the criterion of moral judgements would immediately lead to their murdering their grandmother. Hence that commonplace of accepted mythology, as purveyed by television drama, the character who asserts he is 'beyond good and evil' and proceeds at once to the terribly interesting activity of killing someone. Then again, it is alleged that to cultivate an awareness of the possibility that life might be an illusion would lead inevitably to sudden death under the wheels of the nearest bus.

In short, people claim that they cannot set about cultivating an awareness of the total uncertainty by any method which would involve altering any part of their present attitudes since that would (allegedly) affect their self-preservative abilities.

Accepting this reading of the New Testament remarks, it would appear that Jesus is exhorting everyone to have confidence that the evil results prognosticated would not, in fact, result. But would such an exhortation have any point? Because while, in fact, it may well be that the total uncertainty can be entertained without loss of functionality, it is clearly necessary (in view of the total uncertainty itself) to accept the possibility that it might do so. In fact, it is undoubtedly true that any alteration of attitude which led to a continuous awareness of the total uncertainty might have the most incalculable and far-reaching effects on anybody's life.

*

When Nietzsche said 'Live dangerously', he presumably had the same aspect of existential psychology in mind. I take it, that is, that this is an injunction to live within the emotional context of existential psychology, i.e. in as much awareness as possible of the total uncertainty. Living dangerously in a physical sense is, again, neither here nor there; although perhaps there is some point in exposing oneself to physical risks if doing so appeals to one. I suppose that what does appeal to people in doing so is a certain intensity, rather than, say, identification with the social role of being a racing car driver. But it is difficult to be sure; it is known that people will go to great lengths in fulfilling social roles, and that frequently not the slightest additional awareness of reality results.

*

As an injunction addressed to sane people, i.e. people living within the emotional context in which they are unaware of the total uncertainty, 'Take no thought for the morrow' is meaning-

179

less. It could be said that, living within that context, it couldn't make much difference to their chances from an existential point of view whether they took any thought for the morrow or not, in the sense of exercising some forethought in their material arrangements. But I think I would guess that it would marginally improve their chances of the odd flash of existential awareness if they exercised as much forethought as their peculiar psychological attitudes permitted.

While the operative thing is, of course, the fact of living within the one emotional context or the other, it is quite difficult to imagine anything further removed from existential psychology than the totally irresponsible, totally unforethoughtful social believer.

In the literal, proto-communistic sense, 'Take no thought for the morrow' as a guide to practical interactions with society, is (so far as I can see) nonsense. Taken in the sense of 'Don't think what will become of you if you don't take your exams young', 'Don't think what you will do for money when your present financial support runs out even if you can see that everybody is jigging up and down in gleeful anticipation of the weak position you will be in', etc., it would be lethal.

# CHAPTER 39

# Two Kinds of Psychology

Let us define the purpose of this book.

I am not proposing to offer hypotheses or assertions about the nature of things or the destiny of man.

I am proposing only to define the difference between two opposed orders of psychology. As you know, I call them existential and non-existential psychology respectively. There is no point in concealing my preference.

The point about these two sets of attitudes is that they are coherent within themselves and mutually exclusive. To realise this would save a lot of argument. It is quite unnecessary to argue every point separately; it is only necessary to know which order of psychology a person has adopted.

This follows in the same kind of way as that if a person has a certain number of characteristics typical of an oral or anal personality, you may safely expect others. There is no point in saying (at any rate to a certain type of person): 'Why did you collect small bright objects when you were a child?' and 'Why do you think that people should repay their university grants to the State when they start earning?' as if these questions were not related.

The attitudes of all non-existential people have certain unmistakable characteristics. If any one of these characteristics is present, it is found that all of them are. This is the result of one choice; not many; even though this one underlying choice may have seemed to determine a number of separate decisions about specific things.

\*

The Oxford graduate who had read English and with whom I

corresponded for a time once raised the question of the 'applicability' of my views on human psychology.

I am not quite sure what sort of application he had in mind. I apply my observations on human psychology to account for the fact that they are uninterested in the universe. I find it necessary to try to account for this fact because I find it (a) metaphysically astonishing (b) practically tedious. My views on non-existential psychology (i.e. the psychology of those who are not interested in the universe) have no application to my views on existential psychology. If there were no people in the world who were not interested in the universe, I should not have any views on the psychology of such people, and the absence of such views would not impoverish my mental life.

Chronologically speaking, my explanation of the phenomenon has been augmented as follows.

(1) People are not interested in the universe because they wish to avoid frustration and therefore do not admit to consciousness any drive to the infinite.

(2) In their attempts to create a cocoon of finite omnipotence (by wanting only what they can get) and not to find the result intolerably dull, great emotional valuation has to be attached to concepts involving Society, Other People, Human Relationships, etc.

(3) However, it is important that nothing should ever happen which might remind them of their repressed drive to the infinite. For this reason their 'altruism' breaks down whenever it is confronted by any person or event which reminds them of it.

(4) But on examination, their claims to be altruistically motivated even towards one another break down. Argument on this point is necessarily difficult with anyone who accepts the standard ideas of altruism, since they contain many built-in assumptions. I shall not therefore attempt to enumerate the stages in the analysis which have led to my present conclusion that, in fact, everyone is in a state of profound hostility to everyone else. But you may observe that, if this conclusion be accepted, the system is psychodynamically plausible. We can now see what has become of the repressed drive to the infinite.

I do not usually try to maintain point (4) in argument with sane people. It is obviously invidious. The interest of (3) is rather specialised. I do not argue about it, but I frequently have occasion to demonstrate it in practice.

There is no relation between existential and non-existential psychology. The motivation is different, starting from point (1).

The starting point is that one is interested in the universe. One observes that one is finite and that this is intolerable. One has a limited time and apparently limited capacities with which to find anything out.

Therefore it is possible to despair. There are many orders of despair; and none of them are known to normal psychology. This is demonstrated by the fact that it does not become existential. Normal psychology will never devalue everything.

Existential psychology, at least up to a certain point, consists of exploiting the recoil from the despair of finiteness. The recoil is a drive with at least the instinctive immediacy of the survival instinct. There is no point in saying: 'What is there to do? What could such a drive possibly tend towards?' The survival instinct tends to prolong life; the fundamental drive tends to inform itself about the universe.

# Aphorisms

I have long had a theory that the popularity of Christianity has always depended on its appeal to the sadism of its adherents. The exceptional should be crucified, saith Society; and somehow everyone suspects (in spite of all arguments to the contrary) that if there is a God, he may be exceptional in some way. So the figure of Christ crucified becomes the figure of the dangerous exceptional alien – suitably defeated. 'Only a suffering God can help,' said Bonhoeffer, licking his lips.

\*

People reject the suggestion that Christ was talking about psychological attitudes on the grounds that psychology had not been thought of then. Modern man does not discover truth, he invents it.

\*

*St. Paul:*
The story goes that Christ appeared to him, saying, 'Why are you persecuting me?' – and proceeded to tell him a much more effective way of doing it.

\*

It used to be regarded as a theological problem that God could be indifferent to the continuance of human suffering. What is really remarkable is that the human race can be.

\*

Why do they go on about loving God? It would be much more reasonable to hate him.

*

Prayer is the final dishonesty. You commune with your own psychology and obtain its whole-hearted approval.

*

*'And, in this modern world, seeking God in ordinary life may be as exacting, and indeed may be far more exacting, a task than seeking him in the cloister or the desert.' — Professor E. L. Mascall.*
Carrying water in a sieve is known to be more exacting than carrying it in a bucket. This does not prove it is an equally efficient way of carrying water.

*

Humility means (to the human race) to desire only what you can easily have.

*

It is often suggested that if we thought too much about the 'negative' aspects of the situation (such as our death and finiteness) we should become depressed. Actually this is not the case; depression cannot coexist with the perception of existence. Even ordinary fear is readily distinguishable from depression.

*

In a state of existential awareness, the considerations of normal psychology are easy to remember but appear ludicrous; to normal psychology, the standards of existential awareness seem unreasonably extreme and are easy to forget.

*

The horror is that nobody is seeing the horror.

*

In the world there is nothing but prose and dishonesty.

*

Everyone is encouraged to think more about the needs of others than about their own; this is because it is easier to be unrealistic about other people.

*

Re *the notion that human beings easily want to be God*.

If they think about things it begins to dawn on them that they know nothing; this is a fact, but it makes them feel rather strange so they go and look for something to take their mind off it. Perhaps, like Hume, after too much philosophy, they go and have dinner with some friends.

If that is the measure of the human taste for facts, how can it be imagined that they would at all easily want to be God, which if it means anything must surely mean to know all the facts there are.

*

The sane person pretends not to be egocentric, and pretends not to notice that other people are egocentric, and dislikes people who do not pretend these things. We may suppose that a not-sane person would not pretend these things. He would, for example, be openly concerned at the prospect of his own death, and would allow himself to notice the precise extent to which altruism is actually present in human society.

*

Most descriptions of mystical experiences use the kind of words that one would never spontaneously want to use of anything worth having.

It is rather like the way only insincere people use the word 'sincere'. If you are talking about something really important, you don't have to qualify your attitude as 'a sincere one'. Imagine Einstein, for example, saying: 'My interest in physics is really sincere.' Or anyone saying, 'I have a sincere attitude to death.'

So all accounts of mystical experience are repellent, but descriptions of inspirational states are less so; though usually not in the first person.

*

Sanity has a particular interest in *quantitative* measures. Thus it will argue, 'I am going into hospital but I'm sure I shouldn't let it depress me. One has so few days of discomfort in one's life and one ought to think about the happy times.' It does not, however, argue, 'Only an infinitesimal part of the universe is inhabited by man. Therefore one should not spend a disproportionate part of one's mental energy on the affairs of the human race.'

*

There is a certain prison and a lot of people have been in it for a long time. They won't all be there so very much longer, though, because every so often a few of them are taken away to be executed. But these people are *happy* people, because they have accepted their situation, and they are *interested* in one another. They can never see one another and they can't do anything to help one another, because of course each is locked in his own cell, but they send one another code messages through the walls.

Sometimes a new arrival tries to leave the prison; he is at once assailed by furious rappings from the others. 'Don't you care about my company enough to stay and be executed? How unkind and irresponsible you are.'

*

The most exciting thing possible is actually true.

# Index of Names and Titles

*Some other publications from the Institute of Psychophysical Research are described in the following pages. These are all available through your local book or music shop. In case of difficulty in obtaining any of them please write to: Institute of Psychophysical Research, Oxford.*

## THE HUMAN EVASION

### Celia Green

*The Human Evasion* is an attack on the way of thought of twentieth-century man, revealing the patterns of prejudice which underlie his most cherished and sacrosanct opinions. For all its seriousness, the book is written with sustained wit and intellectual audacity. Surveying the whole field of modern thought, the author reveals the same disease at work in modern Christianity as in theoretical physics. Trenchant and provocative, this book is profoundly controversial – and brilliantly funny.

'Anyone who reads this book . . . must be prepared to be profoundly disturbed, upset and in fact *looking-glassed* himself; which will be greatly to his advantage, if he can stand it. Few books, long or short, are great ones; this book is short and among those few.' – *R. H. Ward*

ISBN 0 900076 02 x

## THE DECLINE AND FALL OF SCIENCE
### Celia Green

A blistering and highly amusing attack on the attitudes of the contemporary scientific and intellectual establishment to psychical phenomena and their investigation. Celia Green relates the refusal to face the problems of paranormal phenomena to the general decline in scientific and intellectual standards within the present century, and this in turn to the impending downfall of Western civilisation. The opening chapters and the aphorisms which begin and end the book contain an epitome of her thought on topics from the psychology of communism to the female image.

'None can fail to acknowledge the brilliance of the author's writing.' — *Hampstead and Highgate Express*

ISBN 0 900076 06 2

# LUCID DREAMS

## Celia Green

Lucid dreams — dreams in which the subject knows that he is dreaming — raise important questions for philosophers and psychologists. If someone can reflect rationally while he is asleep, are we to say he is 'conscious' or 'unconscious'? If someone can critically examine his environment, asking himself whether he is dreaming, and conclude that he is not (although he is), what criterion can we use at any time to decide whether we are awake or asleep?

'A close study, unbiased and precise, of a fascinating subject, together with a wealth of equally fascinating examples.'
— *J. B. Priestley*

ISBN 0 900076 00 3

# OUT-OF-THE-BODY EXPERIENCES

## Celia Green

If someone can perceive his surroundings in an apparently normal way, but from a position which is different from that of his physical body, this is a matter which our theories of sensory perception cannot afford to ignore.

We have also to consider whether someone who has emotional and intellectual experiences while his physical body is unresponsive to external stimuli should be said to be 'conscious' or 'unconscious'; how it is that someone can continue functioning in an apparently normal way while his 'consciousness' is concerned only in watching his movements from an external point; and what evidence for extrasensory perception is provided by the information obtained by the subjects of out-of-the-body experiences.

'The present volume is the first in which contemporary instances are collected, collated and studied . . . the results are extraordinarily interesting, stimulating and well worth examining by the reader.' — *Times Literary Supplement*

ISBN 0 900076 01 1

SCIENCE, PHILOSOPHY AND ESP

Charles McCreery

The phenomena of extrasensory perception and psychokinesis present a disturbing challenge to accepted ways of thought, suggesting that we may need to rethink our attitudes to such fundamental matters as the mind-body problem and the relationship between time and causation.

Charles McCreery's book provides a fascinating introduction to the subject for the general reader. It assumes no previous knowledge of the subject, and numerous examples of both telepathic and psychokinetic phenomena are presented vividly, and discussed in detail.

'. . . A landmark in the history of psychical research. It is a theoretical advance of the utmost importance.' — *Sir George Joy*

ISBN 0 900076 03 8

PSYCHICAL PHENOMENA AND THE PHYSICAL
WORLD

Charles McCreery

A brilliant discussion, with numerous detailed examples, of
extrasensory perception, psychokinesis, out-of-the-body
experiences, apparitions, 'materialisations' and lucid dreams.

'This excellent book cites numerous detailed examples and
discusses the various philosophical questions involved. It
should be of great interest to philosophers, to those concerned with the psychology of perception and, in my opinion, it has implications for the theory of art.' — *Professor Colin
Cherry*

'Alarming clarity. . . . This absorbing book . . . succeeds in
shaking up any comfortable assumptions about the nature
of perception, the perceiver and the perceived in which
the reader may previously have reposed.' — *Times Literary
Supplement*

ISBN 0 900076 04 6

# APPARITIONS

## Celia Green and Charles McCreery

The authors advance the highly original idea that when someone sees an apparition, not only is the figure of the apparition hallucinatory but the whole of the rest of the percipient's environment as well. This novel and at first surprising conception enables them to relate experiences of seeing apparitions to other unusual states of consciousness, notably lucid dreams and out-of-the-body experiences. It also enables them to explain for the first time certain hitherto puzzling features of apparitions, such as the fact that they are usually quite solid-looking and not transparent.

'In my view no one who is interested in the subject should neglect this book.' — *The Rt.Hon. Lord Ogmore, P.C.*

'An excellent piece of documentation, soberly treated, and well worth reading.' — *Anthony Powell, The Daily Telegraph*
ISBN 0 900076 05 4

**MUSIC FOR SOLO PIANO**

Charles McCreery

Grand Sonata in C Major, Op.4

Fifty Variations on an Original Ground Bass in F, Op. 5

Little Waltz in A Flat Major in the Style of Franz Schubert, Op. 6